WHAT ARE THEY SAYING ABOUT
THE PROPHETS?

WHAT ARE THEY SAYING ABOUT THE PROPHETS?

by
David P. Reid SS.CC.

Paulist Press
New York/Ramsey

Nihil Obstat:
Rev. Thomas McElroy, SS.CC.
Censor Deputatus

Imprimatur:
Rev. Msgr. John F. Donoghue
Vicar General for the Archdiocese

February 13, 1980

The nihil obstat and imprimatur are official declarations that a book or pamphlet is free of doctrinal or moral error. No implication is contained therein that those who have granted the nihil obstat or imprimatur agree with the content, opinions or statements expressed.

Library of Congress
Catalog Card Number: 80-80869

ISBN: 0-8091-2304-5

Published by Paulist Press
Editorial Office: 1865 Broadway, New York, N.Y. 10023
Business Office: 545 Island Road, Ramsey, N.J. 07446

Printed and bound in the
United States of America

Contents

Table of Abbreviations

An Bib	Analecta Biblica (Pontifical Biblical Institute, Rome)
B.C.E.	Before the Common Era
CBQ	Catholic Biblical Quarterly (Catholic University, Washington)
HTR	Harvard Theological Review (Harvard Divinity School)
HTRHDR	Harvard Theological Review: Harvard Dissertations in Religion
IDBS	Interpreter's Dictionary of the Bible Supplement volume
JB	Jerusalem Bible
JBL	Journal of Biblical Literature (Society of Biblical Literature)
NAB	New American Bible
OTA	Old Testament Abstracts (Catholic University, Washington)
RSV	Revised Standard Version (of the Bible)
SBT	Studies in Biblical Theology (SCM Press, London)
SDB	Supplement: Dictionnaire de la Bible (Letouzey & Ane, Paris)
TEV	Today's English Version (of the Bible)

TS	Theological Studies (Georgetown University, Washington)
VT	Vetus Testamentum (Brill, Leiden)
ZAW	Zeitschrift fur alttestamentliche Wissenschaft (de Gruyter, Berlin)

Preface

The time has come to hand this manuscript to the publisher. It is a difficult moment, long in coming amid the press of a thousand chores. And yet, it is a welcome moment. I am terrribly aware of the many areas in which this work falls short of the task, and yet I feel the excitement of sharing some insights and new approaches to appreciating the dynamic word of the prophets. The whole adventure has been an edgy experience and this is the hope that goes with it: may the reader be led to the edge and be invited to plunge deeper into the reality of God's ways with humankind. The prophets were very edgy people, rewriting the meaning of today from a perspective on the edge of tomorrow.

Edginess underscores another aspect of this work. While its title employs the word "they," thus referring to what the scholars are saying, this work does not pretend to present the outline and total argument of any one or any number of scholars' works. The attempt has been to weave together a holistic approach to the prophets in dependence on the insights of many

1

scholars, while also offering some original ideas and frameworks. If scholars check this work, they will recognize this indebtedness and will need to critique the utilization made of others' works. I gladly acknowledge my gratitude to the many from whom I draw. Some of the fresh ideas and frameworks presented may engender further scholarly reflection and dialogue.

Edges characterize another aspect as well of this work—its decidedly pastoral approach. Ultimately the word of the prophets is a word to be lived. I believe that all scholarly theological endeavor is directed to interpreting the Word of God into human experience for now. Much in this book has developed out of the experience of ministering to and of having been ministered to by others. Many of the ideas presented have been shared and sharpened in academic courses and with participants in adult education programs and continuing education workshops. The big ministerial test is "will they play in Peoria?" This is not a demand for instant relevance. The question arises from the belief that on deeper reflection the Word of God, addressed to us as it is in the prophets, ultimately promotes common sense. Thus to all those with whom I have shared in searching out the meaning of the prophets, in a very special way my students and colleagues at the Washington Theological Union, I owe a profound gratitude.

This work is not intended to be exhaustive or complete. Its intent is to be provocative and challenging. Something of the prophets' experience must come through in the study of this book. In a word, it may be said that the prophets' answers are not herein claimed to be our answers. However, the prophets' approaches so often recast our old questions that we are challenged to let go of our questions and be searched out in new ones. In asking different kinds of questions, the prophets prevented the Word of God from becoming hackneyed. Thus, the prophets remind us that humankind is ultimately the addressee of God!

On a personal level, I thank Paulist Press for accepting this manuscript and especially the editor of this series and my friend, Rev. Lawrence Boadt, C.S.P., for his encouragement and enthusiasm. I dedicate this work to my parents who embody in my life the questioning edge of the Word of God, who allow me the space to love the question and who selflessly endure my long absences from home in my attempts to answer it.

David P. Reid, SS.CC.
Washington, D.C.
August 1979

Introduction

Prophet in Fact and in Memory

Prophet is one of the many words derived from the Bible employed in everyday conversation. We often hear someone say "so and so is a prophet" or when asked about a possible future happening, one is wont to respond: "What am I supposed to be—a prophet?" Or there is the expectation that one is a prophet if that person is out against the system or the lone individual hammering away on the unresponsive doors of the establishment. Again, we hear the term used to describe one who is particularly insightful. In ecclesial circles, one hears of a prophetic stance being taken by people in ministry or the description of the Religious life in the Church as the prophetic side of the Christian Community.

These examples are very understandable because the prophets are truly the favorite figures of the Hebrew Scriptures, and to be sure, there are some exciting and daring examples of foresight and perseverance in the face of official opposition to be found there. Who hasn't heard the call of Jeremiah or Isaiah being used as an example of readiness to serve the Lord? The New Testament refers very often to the prophets, to the Law and the prophets, to what the prophets had said as being now fulfilled. The description of Jesus as prophet is not uncommon. One might indeed press the issue to ask who in fact were the prophets of the early Church and how do they relate to the prophets of old? This brief overview is enough to indicate two basic perspectives: Who were the prophets and, secondly, what do the Scriptures say about them? When we ask the question which is the title of this book: What are they saying about the prophets? the burden of the answer falls on the second perspective.

We have the historical prophets about whose lives we sometimes know quite a bit, and then we have the words ascribed to them, containing oftentimes many updatings and additions which arose much later than the historical times of the prophets themselves. One might describe this phenomenon in a school catalogue by differentiating between a course on the Prophets and a course on the Prophetic Literature. The proven importance of a figure in the past is often indicated by the welter of material ascribed to his name. A comprehensive study would include then not only a knowledge of the historical prophet, but also the knowledge of the growth and development of the book now ascribed to him. The example of Isaiah, the 8th-century prophet of Jerusalem, jumps to mind. Today scholars date Chapters 40–66 and even some parts of 1–39 as much later than the prophet. These chapters represent another and very different age with a whole set of very different circumstances. The goal of modern scholarship is to trace the continuity and discontinuity contained in the development of this prophetic literature not only as it is ascribed to the one prophet, but also as that development, for example within the Isaian material, is correlated with similar developments in materials assigned to Jeremiah or some other prophet.

There is always the danger of romanticizing the prophets but that danger can be held in check by carefully keeping tabs with the biblical literature about the prophet. We check our own desire to romanticize the prophet by first checking Israel's effort to remember the prophet and apply his message, not forgetting, however, that from time to time Israel no doubt needed to describe the prophet as "bigger than life."

Situating the Prophets

The Hebrew Scriptures comprise three parts: *Torah* (Law), *Nebiim* (Prophets) and *Ketubim* (Writings). The Torah is also known as the Pentateuch, the first five books, and is considered to be the hub about which the other material revolves. The Prophets are presented in two parts: the former prophets comprising what we often call the historical books—Joshua through II Kings—and the latter prophets comprising the three major prophets—Isaiah, Jeremiah and Ezechiel together with the twelve minor prophets. The Writings embrace among other things the wisdom literature. As it stands, this threefold division is helpful and must be reckoned with in any appreciation of the material. Underneath the division one might choose to see the three "offices" in Ancient Israel—the three fundamental forms of ministry—that of the priest, prophet and wise man. Of course, in real life such clean distinctions were not always possible, nor desirable. We know of much overlapping not only in the content and styles of the three divisions of the Hebrew Scriptures, but also in the job description of many a wise man, priest, and prophet. It is modern scholarship which has to be reminded that despite all neat and separate definitions, the priest, prophet, and wise man were all Israelites who worshiped together and promoted their same, if multifaceted, religion. Prophecy, in its turn, was no univocal phenomenon.[1]

Some more distinctions might be helpful here. Prophets are spoken of as pre-classical and classical, the distinction being that the words of the pre-classical prophets were not handed on in separate collections. Of course, what we call pre-classical, the Hebrew Scriptures terms "former." We read of these men and women in the historical books and there they play a vital role in the author's interpretation of Israel's history. If we think of the timeline of Israel's history, the period of so-called classical prophecy is two hundred years plus (750–550 B.C.E.), and the pre-classical period could go back three hundred years before that. Again, we need to distinguish between what we can know of their history and how their memory has been used to depict history as the outcome of the Word of God spoken and acted out through these prophets. This is what makes, for instance, the Elijah-Elisha material (I Kings 17–2 Kings 10) so very powerful. It wasn't just what they did but the stories handed on about them enabled Israel to speak in an expanded, yet concrete way about the "way of God" with God's people.[2]

The terminology "pre-classical" and "classical" might be perceived as prejudicial as if the early prophets were less prophetic than the later ones. It is true that scholarship has tried to impose idealistic theories of historical development upon the data about the prophets using such categories as spirit, cult and ecstasy. This down-grading of the earlier manifestations of prophecy in favor of later classical forms was aligned with a need to show that Israel's religion reached a zenith of development in the classical prophets, leaving behind its lower forms of religious expressions originating with Moses. Today we are very conscious that the latter prophets were not the creators of Israel's religion but rather formulators of its theological, political, and historical ramifications. These prophets stand on the shoulders of their predecessors and many aspects of their teaching and their mode of expression are only understandable in the perspective of the earlier traditions. We need, therefore, to state the meaning of the change from pre-classical to classical prophecy in a way that better reflects the world in which the prophets themselves lived and less based on preconceived theories of historical and religious development of peoples in general.

We can gain great insights into this distinction of former and latter prophets by reflecting on the histori-

cal data of the eighth century B.C.E.[3] Were there not
very different circumstances obtaining then, especially
when one remembers that the interrelationships of
kings and peoples shift a lot in the period just before
the fall of Samaria in 721 B.C.E.? Up to that time the
ministry of the prophets was primarily directed to the
kings of the north and south. One recalls the court
prophets, Gad and Nathan, in the days of King David
and the constant consultation of the prophets on the
part of the northern kings. Perhaps affected by the
new international policy of the Assyrians of dealing di-
rectly with subject peoples, rather than with their
kings, the prophets of Israel direct their words much
more to the whole people—in worship at local shrines,
in the marketplace, at the city-gate during the court of
law, in the vineyards, etc. In a way we might say that
the prophets went "public" when the kings proved
very weak—recall the awful situation on the throne in
Samaria during the ministry of Hosea (2 Kings
15–17)—and in doing so made it possible for a wider
prophetic ministry to take hold, one strong enough to
guide the entire people through the ensuing 150 years
of the sole remaining Jerusalem throne. This going
"public" was a major factor leading to the eventual
collection of the sayings of the prophets and their being handed on from generation to generation.

There developed a self-consciousness about the
prophet and the role which he played. A connection
was perceived between the lot of the prophet and the
fate of Israel, at times clearly etched in the profile of
the king. To tell the story of the prophet was to tell the

tension-filled story of Israel's own history. Jeremiah represents a great turning point here. His confessions show very clearly the inseparableness of the prophet and the people. The actions and life situations of the prophets (e.g., the state of being married, of being a land owner, etc.), speak louder than words. In Ezechiel the surrealism of the Word of God completely dominates the man. As in winter an increasingly heavy fall of snow often halts the normal flow of events and causes us to totally reorganize our schedules, so too the ever-increasing domination of the Word of God spoken through the prophets causes the flow of Israel's history to be rescheduled, that is, converted to the plan of God. The classical period was the crest of the wave—and the falling apart of prophecy in the post-exilic period together with the demise of kingship was not totally unexpected or lamentable. The prophets lived on in memory. They enabled Israel to look back creatively on its holy past. The norm was set to judge the present and anticipate the future. These remarks prepare us to discuss the impact of the prophets on the formation of the Canon of the Hebrew Scriptures. That we will do later. For now let us briefly survey the field of the latter prophets.

It is an emerging conviction of contemporary study of the Bible that a particular prophet is best understood in the light of the expectations which people in that time and place had of the prophet.[4] This is saying more than that we need to know the historical, geographical, economic, and political content. We need to determine the cumulative effect of all these contexts on the expectations, the "contract" of a given prophet. That contract is part of an evolving under-standing and the fresh, creative and untraditional ele-ments introduced by any prophet cause the job description to be rewritten and modified. Although we cannot substantiate the idea that there was a clearly identifiable office of the prophet in Israel, in the cult or elsewhere, nevertheless, we can argue that there was a profile, the sum of many expectations. This pro-file was derived from memory and experience which preceded each prophet and on the basis of which a claim to authority would be based. B. O. Long[5] has written recently on "Prophetic Authority as Social Reality" and detailed some of these expectations which even at times established competing claims to authority. To stake out the ground for classical proph-ecy is to recognize the complex nature of the times and the more intricate nature of the claim to be speaking God's Word. In the early period, the claim of the prophet to speak God's Word often received immedi-ate authentication. The stories of Elijah and Elisha abound with examples of how the prophet spoke and the word was instantly effective. Then the historical conditions of the Neo-Assyrian rise to power and the still later appearance of the Babylonian Empire caused this social expectation of immediacy to give way to an expectation of mediation of prophetic power through remembrance of the prophet's word, even through writing. We will discuss later the meaning of the pow-er of word but for now we can point to even a wider framework. It ought to be remembered that the ultimate designation of Israel's religion as a religion of the book is rooted in this historically conditioned social expectation of the mediated Word of God. This, too, would significantly reshape Israel's understanding of faith and be seen as personal encounter with a God of dialogue through the *aggiornamento* of God's Word in the flow of historical events. The updating of the prophets' words was considered an interpretation of the power in which they inhered and thus were taken as authoritative.[6]

The upshot of these remarks is that classical prophecy is "classical" because of the enormous coming together of all these factors to shape the definition of prophecy in that period. The religious phenomenon of charismatic leadership, ecstatic and otherwise, had been well-known throughout the ancient Near East. In Israel it was being gradually Yahwehized, thus becoming an instrument to help Israel on its historical journey. The dramatic events of the eighth to the fifth centuries B.C.E. impacted heavily on that instrument and caused its further refinement. Prophecy moved from being a somewhat peripheral phenomenon to being central.[7] Its final hour had come. It would leave its indelible mark—a constitutive element—on the religion of the Bible forever and then be gone.

We can group in three stages these dramatic events around which we stake out the terrain of classical prophecy. (1) The second-half of the eighth century (750 B.C.E.) saw the menace of the Assyrian power and the prophetic ministry of Amos and Hosea in the north. In the south Micah and Isaiah offered interpretations of the times too much for the leaders of their day, but happily connected somehow with the reform of the good king, Hezekiah (716–687 B.C.E.). Let us pass over in silence the dreadful reign of Manasseh (687–642 B.C.E.), bad news reported in 2 Kings 21:1–18.

(2) The second-half of the seventh century witnessed the demise of the Assyrians and the rise of the Babylonians, times interpreted in the ministries of Nahum, Habakkuk, Zephaniah and immortalized in Jeremiah. If the immediacy of the Word of God in the ministry of the former prophets began to give way to the challenging mediacy of that Word in the latter prophets that transition found its poignancy in the prophet from Anathoth, Jeremiah.

(3) The third grouping of events can be designated the Exilic and include also the post-exilic prophets: Obadiah, Ezechiel, Haggai, Zechariah and Joel. To this listing we must also add the anonymous authors of Second and Third Isaiah. The historical phenomenon of prophecy had run its course; it was now almost completely a literary phenomenon and in fact two prophetic books—Malachi and Jonah—may represent such a final literarization of the prophetic movement. The word "Malachi" may not refer to a person but to the designation of a prophet as "my messenger" and be a third addition to the book of Zechariah (after Chapters 9–11, 12–14) which was later detached in order to round out the number of minor prophets to twelve. Jonah is a didactic narrative about

a prophet (cf. 2 Kings 14:25) who has become a prov-
erb in his own right.[8]

In conclusion, we recall some of the insights
which come to us when we view holistically the phenomenon of prophecy not only within the history-
bound religion of Israel, but also within that special
outgrowth of Israel's unique religious genius, the phenomenon of the written word, the Bible. Plainly, it
must be stated that what we know of the prophets
comes now to us through the literature generated by
their ministry. This literature is not the container of
their words but the mediator.[9] The very formative processes which came together to give us the prophetic
literature preclude its use as an exercise in antiquar-
ianism. Rather, this literature demands the constant
struggle of faith actualization.[10] Of its nature, the
material is incomplete and its very compilation
grounds a belief in the future.

This observation promotes a pastoral insight. As
mentioned at the beginning of this introduction, it is
not uncommon to hear people referred to as "prophets." Or a questioner often poses the question: Do you
think that so and so is a prophet—Martin Luther
King or John XXIII or Dorothy Day? If I am to answer by pointing out correspondence between Jeremiah of Anathoth, or Isaiah of Jerusalem and the
modern individual, I think I would fail to do justice to
the ground on which the prophets stood, the patterns
of God's-being-with-Israel which jelled in the lives of
the prophets. I cannot afford to compare two points

out of every divergent cultures and times. The prophets were not just individual points along a line but they
together formed and caused to emerge a whole pattern
of expressing the meaning of faith in the process of doing history. It is this pattern of seeking meaning in history through faith which is their legacy and their
enduring constitutive element in the Judeo-Christian
dialectic of Revelation. Let us, therefore, name that
person "prophet" who challenges us to live responsi-
bly in the teeth of history, on the edge of a new tomorrow which we hopefully choose. Such a one embodies
that pattern of living fully in the present out of the future cognizant and enabled by the life-giving traditions
of the past. What would be the point in declaring another "a prophet" if I am not myself put in touch with
the prophetic dimension of my own faith stance of being in the world? And is this not exactly the effect de-
sired by anyone humbled and tried enough not to be
unwilling to shoulder the burden of being named
"prophet"? No prophet was self-appointed and in accepting his own being appointed, he created new possi-
bilities for others to live in faith.

The following chapters will try to delve into aspects already raised in this introduction. The question
of the corporate character of the prophetic witness will
engage us in Chapter one where we will also introduce
some discussion of the modern treatment of the canon
of Scripture. In Chapter two the necessity to penetrate
the symbol of word will be treated and the interplay of
God's Word and the human word will be reflected
upon. "History as Decision" is the title of Chapter

three and runs to the heart of the prophetic faith. This corporate word, filled with the vitality of the one who speaks, is uniquely addressed to humankind in the pots and pans existence of our mortal lives. There are fascinating ways in which the prophets denationalized the Word of God and allowed it to touch the entire gamut of human life as the life of a trusted creature. In Chapter four we will pursue these themes under the cumbersome rubric "from care of the poor to cosmic harmony." In the fifth and final chapter a number of reflections on how to be a prophet without knowing that you are one will be collected under the self-emptying remark of Ezechiel: "thus you will know that a prophet has been in your midst. . . ."

NOTES

1. R. B. Y. Scott, "Priesthood, Prophecy, Wisdom and the Knowledge of God," *JBL*, 80:1–15 (1961).

2. H. W. Wolff, "Prophecy from the Eighth through the Fifth Century," *Interpretation*, 32:17–30 (1978).

3. See J. S. Holladay, "Assyrian Statecraft and the Prophets of Israel," *HTR*, 63:20–51 (1970).

4. B. O. Long, "The Social Setting for Prophetic Miracle Stories," *Semeia* 3:46–63 (1975).

5. B. O. Long, "Prophetic Authority as Social Reality," *Canon and Authority*, Essays in Old Testament Religion and Theology, eds. G. W. Coats and Burke O. Long (Fortress 1977), 3–20.

6. See John H. Schutz, *Paul and the Anatomy of Apostolic Authority* (Cambridge 1975) for an understanding of authority as the interpretation of power.

7. Robert R. Wilson, "Early Israelite Prophecy," *Interpretation* 32:3–16 (1978).

8. Joseph Blenkinsopp, *Prophecy and Canon* (University of Notre Dame Press 1977) esp. Chap. 5.

9. See S. Schneiders "Faith, Hermeneutics and the Literal Sense of Scripture," *TS* 39:719–736 (1978).

10. F. Dreyfus, "L'actualisation à l'interieur de la Bible," *Revue Biblique*, 83:161–202 (1976).

1
The Prophets
and the Prophet

Stating the Question

Amos, the shepherd from Tekoa, is traditionally known as the first of the classical prophets. He is the earliest prophet from whose ministry we have a collection of words ascribed to a given prophet's name. His times were transitional and his words reflect these political, social and religious turning points. In a context of indicting Israel for its serious breach of covenant response, the prophet accuses the people as follows:

> "I raised up prophets from your sons and Nazarites from your young men. Is this not true, sons of Israel—it is Yahweh who speaks, but you have forced the Nazarites to drink wine and given orders to the prophets, 'do not prophesy.' "

> (Amos 2:11–12, JB)

Amos knew well whereof he spoke. He knew the command to speak which came from Yahweh and the countercommand which came from his compatriots. Amaziah, the priest of Bethel, commanded Amos not to speak because his words were causing major upheavals in the community of king and people. In Amos' response, which includes a severe judgment on one (Amaziah) who would set himself against the word of God (7:14–17), we see two dimensions of the ministry of Amos. The first dimension is Amos taking his place among the prophets whom God raises up. "I was not a prophet but God took me." The second dimension is being a minister of the word of God. "And (the Lord) said to me, Go, prophesy to my people Israel." Amos thus owns his position as one among the prophets of the word of God. We might be claiming too much for Amos here. The passage, however, can be taken as a very self-conscious construct on the part of Amos' disciples to offer a retrospective justification as to why the prophet's words should be held onto and listened to.[1] In this perspective our claim would not be untrue to what eventually emerges as a very important element of the accumulated expression of the prophetic self-consciousness: "No prophet is alone."[2]

Hosea also shows concern for the function of the prophets whom he portrays as hearers of the words of God's mouth (6:5). In another text we find:

> "I spoke to the prophets;
> it was I who multiplied visions,
> and through the prophets gave parables."

(12:10 RSV; TEV has "I gave my people
warnings.")

Hosea is known for his freedom in "rewriting" Israel's
historical traditions thus indicating patterns in Israel's
response to God. Whereas Israel has been constantly
failing, the Lord has been consistent in reaching out to
Israel, by sending her prophets; and this fidelity
stretches back to Moses. Thus in Hosea 12:14 it is
said:

> "By a prophet the Lord brought Israel out of
> Egypt and by a prophet they were protect-
> ed."

Are we to understand Hosea as placing himself in a
procession of prophets which reaches back into the
past and thus to Moses?

One final example of this understanding which
prophets had of their relationship to Moses may be
noted from Jeremiah. The opening Chapter of Jeremiah concerns his call to be a prophet. Its composite
character is evident and thus the way is clear to view-
ing the account as a vehicle for reflecting on the religious meaning of his life's work. A number of the
verses anticipate images and actual words in later
parts of the work and verse 9 coincides with Deuteronomy 18:18. The verse reads, "See, I place my words
in your mouth." One is led to reflect on the meaning
of Jeremiah as a new Moses.

These few references to Amos, Hosea and Jeremiah are not exhaustive, but they serve to introduce the insight: no one prophet is enough. It is the accumulated lives of the prophets which contextualize each prophet and out of the total lineup emerges the biblical phenomenon of prophecy. So we have the title of this chapter "The Prophets and the Prophet." This is to begin our reflection on prophets where the phenomenon of prophecy ends, that is, with the cumulative view of prophecy represented in the canon of the Hebrew Scriptures.

The Canon of the Hebrew Scriptures

A static view of how Scripture came about no longer fascinates modern people nor expresses the official teaching of the Church on the matter. The process whereby the Scriptures were assembled as the library of a living and dynamic community has come center-of-stage. Even the image of a library to describe this process may be too static, although it permits us to capture the diversity and plurality of the contents of the Bible. If we could nuance the image of library with the dimension of a living, creative and actualizing memory, then we might come close to a grasp of the contemporary view of the Scriptures. There is no part of biblical study left unaffected by this new and dynamic understanding. Questions about inspiration, interpretation, revelation and canonicity must be left open to this insight.

The image of library is useful for yet another reason. The existence of a library presupposes human exchange and relationship. The recent archaeological findings at Ebla in Syria confirm this observation as we seek the identity, customs and religion of the people behind the artifacts. So often we see today in towns and suburban areas signs which read "Community Library." In itself the title is almost tautological because the one element, library, presupposes and demands the other, community, both for the origin and conservation of the books. Literature presupposes so many life structures needed to facilitate human discourse. When the Hebrew Scriptures are considered as an assemblage of literature, our need to investigate the community which grounds that literary exchange presents itself. Our search can be pushed even further back because the traditions which are now written and organized into a complete unit must be retraced or regained on the pre-literary, oral levels, both in their patterns of origin and convergence. There is in fact always more here than meets the eye! The effort to retrieve the oral levels, where possible, will open up understandings of the community for whom these traditions were their own living, creative and actualizing memories.

The question of canonicity seeks new answers in the light of this process approach.[3] By "Canon," from the Greek word meaning a carpenter's rule, we have always understood the expression of the community's faith awareness which was considered normative for the community. At times, such an expression may have been too bookishly thought of—a charge to which the image of library is also not immune—as a list of writings considered to be inspired. The process of canonization, i.e. declaring certain books to be inspired, was considered too statically as having taken place at one point in time. Critics would automatically question the credentials of the persons who made this canonical listing. The deep meaning contained in the idea of canon could be lost sight of because of the ridicule to which such a static view left the entire matter vulnerable.

In an alternate view which stems from a process understanding of the development of the Scriptures, the central idea stresses that "selective" memory is at work in the making of the canon. When we talk up "selection" rather than "collection" as a way to describe the formation of the Bible, we throw our questioning back to the beginning of the biblical process. Part and parcel of putting into words the significance of the events wherein Israel became, grew and developed as God's people is the process of selection initiated in the ministry of Moses and continued on in the ministry of the prophets. (We are thus restating and expanding the traditional notion that Moses is author of the Torah!) In fact, the Bible presentation of the task of Moses is clarified by reflection on the role of the prophets. Both Moses and the prophets are in the business of selecting Israel's traditions to empower the present generation to move ahead in their history. Their primary task, stated in another way, is to so express the eventfulness of God's presence to Israel as to equip Israel in the present with the freedom to choose the future. This is to place the prophets as the backbone, not only of Israel's religion, but also of the process of canon in the Hebrew Scriptures.

This process of selection can be a model for both the work of the prophets and for the implicity ever-present process of canonization. Selection involves a cutting edge, a choice, a set purpose, a direction. Knowledge of the vast traditions standing behind the prophets[4] will expose us also to the decision-making to which the prophets invited Israel and the direction of the paths which the prophets not only urged Israel to walk but paths which the prophets inaugurated and called into existence. The cutting edge of their message for Israel determines the very shape of the canon. This is so because the appeal of each prophet and his disclosure of God's purpose for Israel is significantly heightened when each prophet takes his place alongside the others. The impact of the prophets on the shape of the canon is to be seen everywhere and thus resembles the overflow of a Baroque painting which cannot be contained within stated borders.

The Pivotal Position of the Torah

Knowledge of the infrastructure of the canon of the Hebrew Scriptures—the law, the prophets and the writings—will disclose the cutting edge and direction built into the enterprise of Israel. The Torah comprised the culled historical traditions of Israel's past ever being updated.[5] This updating could be referred to as the horizontal appropriation of vertical traditions, meaning that a certain pattern of traditions drawn together in the past are applied in new ways to new historical situations. The vertical traditions—of the Fathers, the Exodus, Sinai, the Wilderness—were marvelously drawn together by the theologian(s) of King David's Court, to whom we refer as the *Yahwist* (because of their characteristic denotation of God as Yahweh). There traditions were selectively updated horizontally by the prophetically influenced *Elohist*, the theologians of the North who characteristically referred to God as Elohim.

Two further horizontal appropriations were carried out by the *Deuteronomist* and the *Priestly* authors to meet again the pastoral needs of the people of Israel at major turning points in their history. The Deuteronomic authors retrieved the traditions by placing them anew in the mouth of Moses and setting this speech as introductory to their particular review of the history of Israel. Thus the book of Deuteronomy can be seen as introduction to the former prophets, the books of Joshua, Judges, Samuel and Kings. The Priestly appropriation is a massive reworking of the traditions and supplies the framework and infrastructure of the Torah. Even though these authors are working at a time when the living voice of the prophets is long silenced, nevertheless, one can instantly pick up on the prophetic dimensions of their theology, among other aspects, the themes of the plan of God, the choice, the presence of God, etc. This work is an excellent example of balancing the competing claims to authority in the affairs of God in ancient Israel. The earlier, more prophetically nuanced appropriations are not eclipsed but held in check as it were. It is not the Law or the Prophets. It is the Law and the Prophets.

As called into canonical existence within the perspective of the decision-demanding, accumulated word of the prophets, the Torah then supplies the stuff of the decision to which Israel is called by its very selectivity as canon. What is taking place on the level of literature is exactly what took place in the shrines and vineyards and city gates of Israel. The prophets are calling for fidelity to the covenant made with Israel through Moses.[6] Thanks to the very process of selecting the traditions, nothing of the power of the past is lost; rather, because of a whole host of literary processes, the call of the prophets is even now stronger and more urgent. It is more carefully telescoped, concentrated and impervious to the charge of being merely time-conditioned and an accretion of a by-gone age.

The very process through which the Scriptures were taking their present shape was an exercise in interpreting the Word of God and a call to the people to a faith-filled and decisive appropriation. They were holy books and would "soil the hands" (this is how the ancients referred to the holy books out of a sense of awe; today we might say "this stuff is for real, don't mess with it") not because they were holy of themselves, but because they mediated the living and dynamic word of God, once given to Moses and now present in the Law and the Prophets.

The Canon and Prophets

This question of canon and the crucial impact of the prophets on its development is widely discussed in contemporary scholarship. The term "canon criticism" has been coined to describe the study of the various stages through which the selected biblical traditions passed on their way to canonical acceptance into the canon. Our discussion in these pages has attempted to look at the question as it were *a quo*, whence it came. Others have discussed the question *ad quem*, whither it goes. Joseph Blenkinsopp added recently to this fast developing area of scholarship in a book entitled, *Prophecy and Canon*.[7] Blenkinsopp traces back the roots of the canonical process in the work of the scribes who, with the demise of the Northern Kingdom, began to assemble the traditions of Israel. In Israel's life there had been the two foci of institutional law and prophetic charism. In order to bring the two together in a normative expression of the community's faith, the charism of prophecy had to be changed, adapted, tamed, scribalized. This transmutation made it possible for the presence of the prophetic spirit to continue to be felt at the center of Israel's life. The scribes who carried out this situation of creative tension within the written Word of God would naturally subsume so much of the prophetic presence under their own powerful and bigger-than-life hero, Moses. He now is the prophet from "of old" and the hope for the future is expressed in the expectation of his return. Blenkinsopp studies the continuance of this canonizing work in the Priestly Writers of Jerusalem in post-exilic days and marvelously discusses the organization of the Torah and the Prophets into bodies of writings for the community's guidance.

This sense of tension amidst plurality which finds normative expression in the canon is immensely important for us. We have been already made aware in this century's scholarship that Judaism was not a uniform expression of belief; it embraces many trends, many avenues of thinking and feeling about God. What was often considered the bickering among the Rabbis is in fact a symbol of the "infinite adaptability" of the religious spirit. There are many sides to any one situation, as the "Fiddler on the Roof" would remind us; and the process of using the Scriptures to get a handle on the "adaptability for life"[8] can be dubbed "canonical hermeneutics." J. A. Sanders in his *IDBS* article on hermeneutics speaks of the humor and humility with which we must approach the text. Other recent authors have underscored the necessity to know "the point of view" in any given text. For instance, the "point of view" is crucial to enjoying the humor of the book of Jonah and perhaps also in Israel's claiming its rights from God in Second Isaiah. So much in fact may be tongue-in-cheek that it invites us to turn the other cheek. Truth in the Bible and hence its authority may be much more the new existential horizon dis-

closed before us when we enter on all sides into the
dialogue of historical faith dramatized before us.

Borrowing the language of Paul Hanson[9] we can
say that Israelite theologizing embraced vision and reality and the concomitant struggle to allow both to
have their influence. In a rough way this vision and reality can be paralleled with prophecy-charisma and
law-institution and be said to find expressions in the
ever-awaiting (eschatology) and the settling-in (theoc-
racy) stances of Judaism. It was the marvel of the
prophets to balance vision and reality and this balance
endures in the canon provided we develop a hermeneutic to enter the interplay. As Hanson points out,
there was ever the danger of a retributionist rigor of
the realist on the one hand and the historically-disen-
gaged apocalyptic fantasy of the visionary on the other
hand. In the midst of these options the canon stands as
an instrument of identity and discernment. The community now finds direction for the present in the active and dynamic recalling of the past. The influence
of the prophets is not lost; it remains vibrant and challenging, but the very remembering of the prophets di-
rects Israel's attention to a new and fuller outpouring
of God's spirit. It is thus the active process of canon
that allows the written traditions of the community to
be truly the Word of God.

It has been then the contention of these paragraphs that that process of selectivity and of calling
people to decision-making which crystallizes in the
canon of the Scriptures was indigenous to Israel's reli-

gion from the beginning and received prototypal embodiment in the ministry of the prophets.

Prophecy, a Collaborative Ministry

This wholistic approach to the study of the prophets arising as it does from the theological framework of the Scriptures themselves opens up many areas of reflection. It is an approach appreciated by the prophets themselves as noted in Amos, Hosea and Jeremiah above. In the jargon of our day I would suggest the phrase "collaborative ministry" as a structure within which to arrange some insights on the prophets. The image of group ministry could be applied to the prophets in various ways. It could be used for the bands of prophets who marked the period of Samuel through Amos known as the pre-classical period. One could also search for evidence of later prophets working together, e.g., Isaiah and his wife if we are to take her description as prophetess at face value in Isaiah 8:3. But the perspective which yields an impressive view of the prophetic ministry as collaborative is again the canonical viewpoint. On this level of the Bible's assemblage the prophets speak most powerfully as a corporate witness to the ways of God with humankind over the course of many centuries. The scintillating expression here is "corporate witness." Ezechiel's summation of his own ministry, namely, "they shall know that a prophet has been in their midst" (2:5) could be applied to the entire ministry of the prophets. The message of the canon is that a whole series of prophets has spoken and they constitute by their deeds and words the stuff of Israel's religious life.

To speak thus of the corporateness of the prophets flies in the face of any view of the prophet as the lone individual over against the institution. We cannot exclude, to be sure, some very singular and distinctive traits to be found in individual prophets. In fact, we will argue later in this work to the necessity of such individuality in regard to the symbol of the Word. However, the point being made here is this: no one prophet is enough; rather we must recognize the radically collaborative structure which the prophetic ministry exhibits on a closer and unprejudiced examination. There are two factors here, which are distinct but inseparable.

The first factor is that all ministry by definition is the struggle to articulate in language, and thus set in patterns, the experience of encounter with God. This process of giving language to the event of God is disclosed by the prophets to be at the heart of Israel's theologizing. We shall expose dramatic examples of the prophets pushing Israel to very new and revelatory articulation of newly discovered faith. But as often as the prophets did such things, they were rehandling the language, the sacred traditions of the community. Language is a social reality; it belongs to the community and the prophets' rehandling of it was all the more powerful because they were not outside the social unit. They were one with the community.

The second factor is the contingent historicality of Israel's faith-relatedness with God. Israel's religion started and continued on within given historical and social frameworks and there is no escaping having to deal with the language which these frameworks supply. Recent scholarship has issued many salutary cautions against claiming too much distinctiveness for Israel's faith in a God of history.[10] However, we can speak of that faith being born out of the many encounters of Israel with God through the subsequent reflection on past events. While Israel is not alone in seeing its God work in history on its behalf, nothing in the ancient world compares with the normativization of a certain series of those events as we find for instance in Deuteronomy 26 or Psalm 78. But to see and maintain this pattern of continuity amidst discontinuity, to structure experiences in the pattern of covenant and promise, demands a collaborative structure of pregnant memorializations.

The prophets were pastors. They helped Israel to put language on its experiences, that is, they helped to interpret Israel's reality. They were Israel's creative, living, challenging and actualizing memory. They gave unity and direction to Israel's sojourn through many vicissitudes. They lent words to the passions of God and in their search for meaning they related in a whole host of ways the deeds of history and the words of God. If Revelation can be spoken of in terms of the interplay of words and deeds,[11] then the prophets are paradigmatic in their art of reciprocal interpretation.

By undoing so many of Israel's smug interpretations—pulling the rug from under its feet—the prophets provided Israel with the space to be encountered by God.

NOTES

1. See G. Tucker, "Prophetic Authenticity: A Form Critical Study of Amos 7:10–17," *Interpretation* 27:423–434 (1973).

2. R. Rendtorff, "Reflections on the Early History of Prophecy in Israel," *History and Hermeneutic*, W. Pannenberg et al. (Harper and Row 1967).

3. D. N. Freedman, "The Canon of the Old Testament," *IDBS*, 130–136.

4. W. Zimmerli, "Prophetic Proclamation and Reinterpretation," *Tradition and Theology in the Old Testament*, ed. D. A. Knight (Fortress 1977) 69–100.

5. W. Brueggemann and Hans Walter Wolff, *The Vitality of Old Testament Traditions* (John Knox 1975).

6. W. Zimmerli, *The Law and the Prophets: a Study of the Meaning of the Old Testament* (Harper and Row 1967).

7. Joseph Blenkinsopp, *Prophecy and Canon* (University of Notre Dame Press 1977). This work has been favorably reviewed (*CBQ* 40:598–600, 1978) by James A. Sanders, a veritable pioneer in this field. See his *Torah and Canon* (Fortress 1972).

8. James A. Sanders, "Adaptable for Life: The Nature and Function of Canon," *Magnalia Dei: The Mighty Acts of God* (Festschrift G. E. Wright) eds. Frank Moore Cross, Werner E. Lemke, and Patrick D. Miller, Jr. (Doubleday 1976) pp. 531–560.

9. Paul Hanson, *The Dawn of Apocalyptic* (Fortress 1975).

10. See B. Albrektson, *History and the Gods* (1967) and James Barr, "Revelation in History," *IDBS* 746–749.

11. Document on Revelation, *Dei Verbum*, Vatican II.

2
The Vitality
of the Word

What's Behind a Word?

The previous chapter concerned itself with reflections which arise when we consider the place taken by the prophets in the canon. It is a case of the one and the many, the prophet and the prophets. Are there connecting bonds between the actual life of an individual prophet and the distillation in canonical shape of his words? Our task in this chapter is to reflect on the connecting bond and already we have hinted as to what that really is: the vitality of the Word. There is less danger of losing sight of the historical prophet in the Old Testament than there is of losing sight of the historical Jesus in the New Testament.[1] But just as in the historical Jesus-Christ of faith discussion, a methodology of continuity and not juxtaposition is necessary, so too in the prophets/prophet discussion a methodology founded on the vitality of the word is necessary.

Much has been written about the meaning and power of the spoken word in Israel. Unfortunately, an angle has been gained on the discussion only by downgrading our modern experience of the human phenomenon of the word. It is unfortunate because, while we must admit that words have lost some of their potency in their incredible mass production today, we by no means totally lack an appreciation of the force and dynamism of the human word, whether written or oral. The President's signature can turn a bill into a law binding on all citizens, or another document into a history-making resignation or pardon. The simple "I do" as part of a marriage ceremony can inaugurate and sustain a lifetime of committed togetherness for a woman and a man. The sheer facility in producing words today has gradually cautioned us to be immensely circumspect as to sources. This last remark brings us to consider what was the real focus of the ancients' fascination with the word: the identity and the power of the speaker or writer.

"Dynamic" and "dianoetic" are two terms used in the scholarly discussion to describe this phenomenon.[2] By dynamic is meant the power and force of the person who speaks, and by dianoetic, the self-revelatory output of the speaker. The prophetic claim of the authority of God in one's words was to claim the release of the power of God into human life and to reveal something of the "personality" of God. Such was indeed the claim of the prophets and if their claim was verifiable, then their words were inevitably productive. We noted earlier the reaction of Amaziah to Amos.

No attempt was made to deny his words; rather, there was an attempt to remove him from the scene and thus block his judgment-launching words.

The Prophets as Speakers

The prophets were primarily speakers of God's words. Among the classical prophets only Second Isaiah appears as a possible exception and even then his words may have arisen in part from the prophet's participation in lamentation services in the Exile. The discussion of the character of the prophets' original utterances is helped much by the findings of form criticism, the science which seeks to understand the prophets speaking in their original social and historical setting. In this branch of biblical exegesis many other factors come into play and one can conjecture as to the timing, occasion and the audience of a particular pronouncement and especially the rehandling by the prophet of long-accepted and well-established speech forms. This discovery that the prophets were primarily to be thought of as speakers underlies the great advances made in modern scholarship on the prophets. Although today we do not think that the original prophetic utterance was a short opaque enigmatic statement as some contended in earlier studies, nevertheless, the biblical material does not permit us to imagine the prophets giving long-winded speeches. The longest units which are distinguishable as such are not long by our standards of speech making. Not very much is said in the Scriptures about the prophets' symbolic actions, but should we suppose that much of the speech of these messengers of God was accompanied by easily comprehended body talk? Elijah and Elisha were clearly recognized as important men of the Word of God. The stories devoted to them are legendary developments of this perceived importance. Far less attention is given to their words than to the dramatic and enigmatic dimensions of their character.

The symbol of the word to denote the divine human exchange has far-reaching ramifications.[3] How is one to interpret the expression, "God speaks"? Is the emphasis on God speaking or on the human hearing? Perhaps, the latter. The symbolism of the word is very effective because it designates a personal communication that reaches to the interiority of the other person. When God is said to speak, does that expression indicate that the prophet hears an already articulated word in his or her ear? Or does the expression indicate that the prophet so experiences the presence of God as to suggest a particular interpretation by the prophet on the basis of the hearer's personal appropriation of the traditions of the community? Can we hear another's word without feeling his breath? Does the prophet experience the breath of God? Can there be an experience of the Word of God which is not also an experience of the Spririt of God? An earlier scholarship was concerned to sort out the ecstasy—whether of concentration or absorption—in which the prophet received the communication. At times this discussion seemed to flow from an understanding that the Word of God was spoken in already clearly-articulated human language. The prophet would have been merely a mouthpiece of God, and, in fact, this image of prophet influenced the discussion of biblical inspiration.[4] Even staying within the phenomenon of ecstasy, the question is more properly asked: What does the prophet experience and how much of what he or she says is interpretation of this experience in the language of the community and in the light of his or her own reading of the signs of the times?

On the one hand, speaking of the prophet as experiencing God will seem to many readers as imprecise and inadequate to control. On the other hand, a deeper knowledge of the social nature and obvious community orientation of the language used by the prophet precludes thinking of the prophet as a receiver of already assigned language in the mode of a mouthpiece. Perhaps, we have reached an impasse in trying to tie down the interior experience of the prophet. There are many prophets. If we are not to force a uniform and previously designated model of prophetic inspiration on them, then, perhaps, we ought first to know something of the individuality of a given prophet, the points of intersection of his/her spirituality with life experiences and from there develop a working model with which to view all the words and events associated with that person. Thus, for example, in studying Hosea we touch base with a man of immense sensitivity of things human and divine. This deeper experience of the paths of God both illuminated the prophet's personal life as well as exposing to him the harlotry in the social, political and religious spheres of Israel's life. In the prophet Isaiah we touch base with a man of immense political acumen which illuminated by the gift of faith equipped him to interpret the international and domestic scene of his day. In Ezechiel, we encounter the soul of a surrealist who could embody the unnatural juxtaposition of a God of intense and passionate love and the inveterately rebellious and stubborn resistance of Israel even in its last hour. Any working model must begin then by noting the prophet's spirituality based on human and religious experience.

The focus of the discussion about the prophet's consciousness has shifted often in the history of research. The message he first fashions endures after the messenger is long dead and becomes part of the community's heritage in faith. It attains to literary and canonical expression. But its vitality is forever present and one can never forget the sources of that vitality in the personalism of Israel's religion as it is both embodied in and refined through the prophetic ministry. The prophet represents the interplay of the community and the individual, the interfacing of a person's experience of God and the accumulated tradition of the community whenever that personal experience is allowed to refashion and heighten the community's traditions.

The Prophet and the Fate of God's Word

The prophet stands wholly on the side of God. A major surrender is demanded and the resistance to the message which the word would encounter was not unknown to the messengers. The word shapes the very life of the prophet in the cases of Isaiah, Hosea and Ezechiel, in the matter of their married lives and in the case of Jeremiah in his not being married. The prophet can never be outside the process of ministering to God's Word. He or she is rather the interior facilitator of that word which brooks no opposition. To speak of the "interior" facilitator is to note that the prophet was not just an external agent, a "have" as opposed to the have-nots. There was just no room for cool, detached objective observers. The call narrative of Isaiah reminds us of the conversion through which the prophet passed before he could hear the council of God in session. His lips had to be purged. He was one of the many people to whom he was sent. His call is one with the Word of God which he must address to his fellow Jerusalemites.

The prophet runs the risk of death, should he try to quench the word within him; better not to have been born than to resist the power of the word within his breast! The Word became his lot in life and the opposition to God's Word made a passion narrative of the prophet's human existence. The fierce awesomeness and power of God was tearing away on the insides of the messenger and attempts to renegotiate the terms of his commissioning ended in the prophet's being recommissioned. Jeremiah comes to mind immediately as the bearer of the fate of God's Word. There is no neutral ground in face of the revelation of God. Jeremiah could not resist preaching the Word. One could not live with the Word nor live without the Word. Indeed, Amos had once warned Israel that its punishment would be a famine of the Word of God (8:11).

This discussion of the Word of God in the prophet's life presents a context out of which we can briefly reflect on 1) Ezechiel's understanding of his ministry; 2) the phenomenon of false prophecy; and 3) the role of the suffering servant in Second Isaiah.

1) In Ezechiel 2:5 we read "Whether those rebels listen to you or not, they will know that a prophet has been among them." The prophet is assured that when the right time comes, the people will recall that the prophet had spoken. Thus, the events which the people have undergone were planned and, in fact, set in motion by the ministry of the prophet. This will be so whether the people resist or heed that ministry. A careful study of the context of this verse will show that this call story of Ezechiel, assembled most probably by his disciples, follows a pattern found quite often in the Hebrew Scriptures and especially the prophets. One of the enigmas of Isaiah's call story is that resistance to his preaching and the ultimate failure of his word seems assured beforehand (6:9–10) and the attempt to soften the impact of this statement by declaring it "a posteriori" is unwise. This theme of resistance shows up elsewhere, for instance, in the so-called biographical material on Jeremiah where so often we see the king's resistance to God's Word directed against the person of Jeremiah. What Ezechiel's statement so clearly displays shows up then in many other places and one could document this in the former prophets

also. This discussion of patience in the face of resistance leads us to our second point.

2) In retrospect, it seems terribly easy to decide who were false and who were true prophets. Of course, the perspective of centuries allows us that luxury and even allowed the Greek translators of the Hebrew Scriptures to interpret some as having been "pseudo" prophets.[5] The Hebrew writers did not so designate any prophet. The facile approach of the Book of Deuteronomy in setting up its criteria comes across as very stilted, contrived and as Monday morning quarterbacking. However, knowing the complexity of the human events in which the prophets were engaged, we may not be off the mark to suggest that the so-called true prophets held their fingers crossed as they said what they claimed to be God's interpretation of a given human predicament. In the heat of controversy and turmoil the question was not easily resolved. We can go back in spirit to the ten-year period 597–587 B.C. and hear the many arguments going on in Jerusalem as to the chances of a further rebuff to the Babylonians and the projections as to the length of the Exile. The scene in Jeremiah 28 is made up of two characters, Hananiah and Jeremiah. The former came equipped with the century-old theology of Isaiah, but Jeremiah felt constrained to reject his facile assurance of deliverance. Jeremiah's responses are informative. Hananiah did not have the precedent of the prophets in his favor, Jeremiah declares, and so the burden of proof is on the prophet who would proclaim peace. It was the popular message and would meet no opposition. In 28:9 Jere-

miah notes, however, that a prophet of peace is truly recognized as sent by the Lord only when his word is fulfilled. In verse 15 another criterion for authenticity is brought forth. "The Lord has not sent you" and "you have raised false confidence in this people." Does Jeremiah know more than his readers? Or are we face to face with the painful struggle of being a prophet, combatting others and yet hoping that one is not completely off target himself? To overcome even one's own resistance to the Word of God and be willing to live with that ambiguity in faith and trembling hope of being vindicated, perhaps long after one's own death? It was always so easy for a prophet to pick the easier route, say something to please the crowd and rescue people from the implications of their own sinfulness. Hananiah broke the wooden yoke, worn by Jeremiah, as a symbol of the release from captivity which he declared to be immanent. Some time later Jeremiah declared that God would replace the wooden yoke with an iron yoke. Such ambiguity is central to a historical, earth-bound revelation. It would be too clever to depict the issue as a struggle between the good guys and the bad guys. The prophet must rather wait out in patience and perseverance even the conflicting interpretations of all the prophets. That prophet is true who serves even without winning a stroking from God, sets his or her ministry openly and translucently at the service of all and sees the resistance sustained as eventually cleaning the air and revealing God's plan even long after the prophet himself has left the scene. As Jeremiah was so often reminded, it was a task for which God's strength alone sufficed. The prophet would be one who served open-endedly. God alone reveals the true prophet and this initiates the discussion of our third point.

3) The material in 2nd Isaiah known as the Suffering Servant songs, has always presented a challenge to interpreters. Scholars do not only argue on the extent of the poems, but also on problems of authorship, origin and identification of the servant. However, the perspective offered in considering the prophet as bearer of the lot of the Word of God throws new light on old and vexing questions. If the suggestion made above holds true, namely, that the true prophet is one who bears the burden of the word in patience and perseverance, then we have a kind of background over against which to evaluate the reflection on prophecy contained in the songs. Our understanding would be that these poems represent a theological construct of the meaning of Israel in the plan of God. The servant is Israel, depicted on the canvas of prophecy, as fully embodying the plans of Yahweh. The many stories which Israel cherished about the prophets and how they suffered the lot of the word furnished the author of Second Isaiah with the material needed to fashion this reflection on the meaning of Israel in God's plan. In the passage 44:24–28, which can serve to sum up the entire message of Second Isaiah, the prophets are called servants in parallelism with messengers (verse 26), and many times within the context of Second Isaiah, Israel is called servant. The denouement of the Exile has caused a redefinition of Israel to emerge. The

suffering is no mere punishment for sin but an entering into solidarity with God's plan of saving love, the horizons of which plan reach now beyond Israel and are universalized (understood as subordination of all the nations to Israel). It might only be a form of pride for Israel to consider its suffering as punishment for sin. Not unlike Isaiah, Israel has been purged and prepared for a task of universal and cosmic proportions. Israel has finally bowed its head in a slavery of liberation.

Within the old framework of retribution, one who suffers has sinned. Could it be that one who suffers, loves? So suffering admits of diverse interpretations and one who embodies God's love may have to endure the ambiguity of such interpretations. More difficult to bear than physical suffering is the burden of being misinterpreted and yet carrying that burden is the stuff of the true prophet of the Word of God. Second Isaiah is very clear as to the source of the servant's suffering. "The Lord laid upon him the guilt of us all . . . and the will of God shall be accomplished through him" (53:6,10). Israel is ideally depicted, standing wholly on the side of God, willing to endure the false interpretations to which suffering gives rise and thus in solidarity, offering to all who suffer the caring and the loving of the one God of Israel and all the nations.

NOTES

1. See G. Stanton, *Jesus of Nazareth in New Testament Preaching* (Cambridge University Press 1974), for a balanced approach.

2. J. L. McKenzie, "The Word of God in the Old Testament," *Myths and Realities* (Bruce 1963), 37–58;
Bruce Vawter, "God Spoke," *New Paths through the Bible* (Dimension 1968), 127–140; F. Moriarty, "Word as Power in the Ancient Near East," *A Light unto my Path: Old Testament Studies in Honor of Jacob M. Myers*, H. Bream, R. Heim, Carey Moore, eds. (Gettysburg Theological Studies 4; Philadelphia: Temple University Press), 345–362.

3. For discussion of this material see G. von Rad, *The Message of the Prophets* (Harper & Row 1962), esp. Chap. 5 entitled, "The Prophets' Conception of the Word of God," also J. Lindblom, *Prophecy in Ancient Israel* (Fortress 1962).

4. See Bruce Vawter, *Biblical Inspiration* (Westminister 1972) esp. Chap. 1.

5. The significance of the "false prophets" is pursued on many levels. For a discussion of the contemporary state of scholarship see J. Crenshaw, *IDBS*, 700–702; also J. A. Sanders, "Hermeneutics in True and False Prophecy," *Canon and Authority*, 21–41; The section in L. Ramlot, "Prophetisme," *SDB*, VIII (1970) cols. 811–1222, dealing with false prophets, esp. cols. 1040–1050.

3
History as Decision

To the Future

    Gene M. Tucker reviewed recent developments in the study of the language of the prophets. His article concludes with a very insightful statement: "Fundamental to the prophetic role in Israel was the utterance for the future."[1] At first glance, this statement made by Tucker may seem to be a simple assertion of what is commonly thought about the prophets: they foretell the future. Although it must be admitted that something of the customary understanding of the prophet as one concerned with the future still holds good in modern scholarship, however, in no way is such a facile view to be derived from Tucker's research.

    Yes, the prophet is very concerned with the future, in fact, is totally absorbed in what we might call "the future of God." But he or she is no clairvoyant. The prophet's task is not to pick off the events of the future as if shooting at beer cans placed on a wall. No doubt a caricature! The point to be stressed here is that such a view of the prophet would be too extrinsicist an understanding of how God chooses to work with humankind in history. An example of this extrinsic grasp of the matter is often found in how the connection between the Old and New Testaments is discussed. There is a kind of counting up of the number of prophecies in the Old Testament fulfilled in the New Testament. Thus, a bridge of promise/fulfillment is established. This approach is much too mechanical and deprives us of appreciating Israel's prophets in all the pain, doubt, ambiguity and *ad hoc*-ness of their ministry. This approach divorces the prophet from the present in which he lived. It obscures the very ground for the appreciation of the future which future is seen by the prophet as flowing from the moral content of the present. The future for the prophet is not the "long shot" which could or could not be, but which is now magically announced ahead of time. Rather, the future is the organic outreach of the religious decisiveness with which the Israelites choose to own their own turf in the present. In order to penetrate the prophet's understanding of that which we term "future" we must first delve into their concept of time and event.

Time

It will sound tautological to say there are times and there are times, but yet our own experiences clearly confirm the point that life is made up of many clearly distinguishable times. There is time reckoned by the motion of the heavenly bodies and counted on the face

of the clock or the digital watch. Time can be over-ca-
lendarized, frozen, made into slots of hours and min-
utes and stretched like a carpet into the projections of
tomorrows, the commonly accepted definition of future.[2] Time, too, can be filled with waiting and hope
and promise, memory and imagination, healing and
resurrection. In Israel's prayer and worship, the moments of God's closeness were relived and, thus, the
hope of God's faithfulness to the covenant undergirded so much of Israel's repentance and desire for God's
forgiveness. Ordinary life was lived in the hollows of
time between the great feasts to be celebrated on the
hill of Jerusalem. There, time was encounter, filled
with the presence of the other. A thousand years elsewhere did not compare with a moment in the presence
of the Lord on Zion. Time could also be counted in the
movement of the seasons and the annual cycle of nature. All of life came magnificently together when a
person bore the first fruits of his toil to the temple of
God. It was felt that the personal presence of God experienced in nature found its ultimate expression in
the covenanted presence of God in worship and thus
enriched the symbol of time entirely. Nothing com-
pared with the cultic moments of festival celebration
when the community and choir sang antiphonally of
the great deeds that the Lord had done on the entire
people's behalf to ground the symbol of time in the experience of God. Time was the movement, the dynamism, the personal presence of a God whose word
endures forever and whose love is everlasting (see Ps.
136).

Time and Promise

From Israel's beginning the experience of its God was articulated in terms of promise. Their wandering Aramaean forefathers, the patriarchs, ever in fear of perishing and thus, ever on the move for arable land, believed deeply in a clan God of promise. It is fascinating to see how the twin factors of time and promise intertwine about the motif of journeying. The God whose experience gave substance to their concept of time was known as the "one who led us" out of the house of slavery, Egypt, and brought them into a land flowing with milk and honey. Not only is Yahweh a God of promise, but Yahweh is one to whom appeal could be made on the basis of known fidelity to promises. For Israel there would be a future because theirs was a God of proven fidelity. If the experience of the presence of God with his people grounded the promise of encounter, that encounter could mean salvation or judgment. Perhaps, nowhere in the prophets' material is the advent of God more stridently stated than in Amos 4:12, "Prepare to meet your God, O Israel." The prophets experience deeply that God is coming in judgment and seeks to relate that coming to the present. In how the people respond ethically to the demands of God in the present, they prepare to receive the future which God's coming to them constitutes. Or stated another way: the prophets experience the advent of God in judgment against Israel. Assured as they are of this fact, they announce it to the people. They seek to find in the people's conduct why it is that

God comes to judge. God's fidelity was not then a to-
be-taken-for-granted, rubber stamp kind of fidelity.
God's promise to come was as strong, unequivocal and
as all creative of futurity as God's jealousy was expres-
sive of God's unity. God's fidelity could not be di-
vorced from God's oneness so that God could not be
played off against God.

Promise and Present

The prophets receive the news that God is coming in different ways. Amos, the shepherd from Tekoa,
assumes a traditional role for the prophet and tries in-
terceding for the people. But alas, he must bow to the
inevitable. Then he sets about demonstrating the
sources of Israel's evil-doing. As Martin Luther King
pointed out in his famed "Letter from a Birmingham
Jail," the prophets went to the very source of Israel's
sinfulness. Amos is not content to point to sin, "You
who oppress the weak, and abuse the needy;" but
touches base with the reason for this activity in "who
say to your lords 'Bring drink for us!' " (4:1). Greed
and gluttony bring on sins of social injustice.

Jeremiah has left us a heart-rending insight into
his experience of the advent of God. In describing the
invasion from the north which the prophet obviously
uses as a symbol of God's coming judgment, Jeremiah
says:

"My breast! My breast! How I suffer!
The walls of my heart!

My heart beats wildly,
I cannot be still;
For I have heard the sound of the trumpet
the alarm of war.
Ruin after ruin is reported;
The whole earth is laid waste.
In an instant my tents are ravaged; in a flash,
    my shelters.
How long must I see that signal, hear that
    trumpet sound!" (4:19–21)

Jeremiah was devastated by the word he had to speak, the kind of future already in his gut which he had to announce. Like Amos, Jeremiah clearly identified the source of Israel's sinfulness in the present which related to this ominous future. The very next verse in Chapter 4 after the verse cited above describes the people:

"Fools my people are,
they know me not;
Senseless children they are,
having no understanding;
They are wise in evil,
but know not how to do the good."

The prophet identifies at the core of the people's religiosity a structure of deceit,[4] showing up in many spheres. There were many areas where over-confidence was had. We can single out the temple and recall Jeremiah's word in Chapter 7:4, "Put not your trust in the deceitful words: 'This is the temple of the Lord! The temple of the Lord! The temple of the Lord!' "

The verses which follow spell out the deceit contained in the words. They are empty because the people show no concern for the demands of God—the case of the resident alien, the orphan and the widow— and only on condition of the people's thorough conversion will the Lord remain in this place. Verse 7 recalls two covenants: made with David and made with the fathers to whom Yahweh had given the land long ago. The fulfillment of the promise of the Lord of the future is tied in to the people's ethical response in the present. It is the prophet's task to pinpoint the moral continuity or threaten the moral discontinuity between the present and future. Both the tragedy of sin and the joy of a turn-about are found in the prophets' juxtaposing human moral discontinuity and the loving divine continuity of an ongoing creation.

Salvation was also promised by the prophets. It is important to note this reality because the people's non-response was not allowed to become the protagonist on the stage of the Yahweh-Israel drama. The prophet not only announced, or at times described, this salvation, but also added the purpose for this turn in events.[5] It was not because the people had repented. Rather, it was the freedom to be a loving God which marked Yahweh's relationship to the people. If the prophet's preaching of repentance seemed to promote a stuffy principle of retribution, the disclosure of God's intended salvation disproved the adequacy of such a principle. In Second Isaiah, salvation is provided in none other than the self-identification of Yahweh—"I am the Lord, your God who grasps your right hand: It is I who say to you, 'Fear not, I will help you'" (41:13). The prophet Ezechiel penetrated the deepest purpose of God's salvation and abruptly stated it as follows: "Not for your sakes do I act, house of Israel, but for the sake of my holy name" (36:22). One is reminded of the rather curt expression of Hosea (11:9):

> "I will not give vent to my blazing anger,
> I will not destroy Ephraim again,
> For I am God and not man,
> the Holy One present among you;
> I will not let the flames consume you."

We see, then, that it is the kindness of God with the people which grounds the future. Staying with Hosea for a minute, we can read Chapter 14 where a penance service seems in process. It begins with the invitation to return and verse 3 reads: "Take with you words, and return to the Lord." Although it is difficult to know the meaning of "take with you words," it seems clear that for the prophet, the future is chosen in response to a God who refuses to be dictated to by human sin.

History and the Future

The German scholar, H. W. Wolff, has given a profound definition of history which helps us to know

the prophet's conception of the future. He speaks of
history as the "goal-directed conversation of the Lord
of the future with Israel."[6] What is so helpful in this
definition is the stress on the word "conversation" and
the dialogue character. Not only in the past did God
take the initiative (see Exodus 19:3), but there will be a
future beause God is goal-directed in the dialogue with
Israel. The people's response in this conversation is depicted in the very personal symbol of the word as discussed earlier. The future flows from that series of
decisive turnings to the Lord and appropriating of
God's plans which are part and parcel of one's response to the Word, addressed by the prophet to the
very heart of the nation.

We can speak of decision-history in this regard
because the necessity for wholehearted response in the
present is thus more fully emphasized. We can introduce the setting for this decision-making by first noting a very strange thing which happened in Israel. To
get a handle on this occurrence we return by way of
detour for a moment to the second commandment of
the Decalogue. Exodus 20:4 reads:

> "You shall not carve idols for yourselves in
> the shape of anything in the sky above or on
> the earth below or in the waters beneath the
> earth."

Exegetes have noted the problem whether the idols
hereby proscribed are idols of Yahweh or of other

gods. The confusion comes with the "them" in verse 5. I would suggest reading verses 3 and 5 together and referring the "them" to the other gods, of whom the Israelites are to have none. Verse 4 then would stand on its own and refer, I suggest, to the prohibition of idols of Yahweh. Are we to say, then, that Israel's religion was bereft of images? No! How could a human religion be without images? But what Israel's image will be is the symbol, the creed of the great events which God has wrought on its behalf. When Israel came to worship, the people recited the creed to tell God the story of his love for them. Each worship-filled telling demanded decision. It was an awesome reality to pray that recital and commit oneself all over again to so power-filled and holy a God.

The strange thing that happened was that even these creeds became grounds for overconfidence and indifference to the demands of the covenanted relationship. The people seemed to think that just recital of the creed without inner commitment to the ethical demands of the Lord Yahweh would ensure blessings. The prophets reacted with a creativity and a recklessness which must have astounded their hearers. In many prophets, we have examples of this reversal of the traditions which collapse the past and the future into the immediacy of the present time, this encounter, now today! The very creeds which the people made into expressions of arrogance and over self-confidence, the prophets cited as reasons why the people should be condemned.

As is the case so often, we have in the book of

Amos a very striking example of this reversal. Amos
3:1–2 represents a programmatic introduction into
Amos' collection and the verses read as follows:

> "Hear the Word, O men of Israel
> that the Lord pronounces over you,
> over the whole family that I brought up
> from the land of Egypt.

> "You alone have I favored,
> more than all the families of the earth;
> Therefore, I will punish you
> for all your crimes."

Verse 1 clearly reminds Israel that Israel is not its
own, but is what it is because of Yahweh's elective
love. Verse 2 drives home the message in the use of the
word "therefore" and the very terse "for all your
crimes." The traditions of election which Israel had
used to bolster its confidence in itself and before God
received a classical put-down in the mouth of Amos.
We read in 9:7–8: "Are you not like the Ethiopians to
me, O men of Israel? says the Lord. Did I not bring the
Israelites from the land of Egypt? As I brought the
Philistines from Caphtor and the Arameans from Kir?
The eyes of the Lord God are on this sinful kingdom. I
will destroy it from the face of the earth."

Again, it is wise to comment on the message of
salvation promised in the prophetic message. It was
more difficult to promise salvation because the messenger could be so much more easily misled, and, in

fact, prophets of salvation often caused confusion and pain. However, the known experience of God's relation with the people was also the ground of this hope. The future was described in images of the past and one recalls perhaps the greatest example of this in the New Exodus imagery of Second Isaiah. However, it must be clear that the creeds from the past were not the source of literal descriptions of God's future action. They merely indicated the God who promised salvation and healing. There may well be helpful analogies from the past, but God's future was always something new and surprising.[7]

NOTES

1. G. Tucker, "Prophetic Speech," *Interpretation*, 32:31–45 (1978).

2. See G. von Rad's discussion in *The Message of the Prophets*, Chap. 6, "The Origins of Hebrew Thought about History."

3. John Bright, *Covenant and Promise* (Westminster 1976).

4. Thomas Overholt, *The Threat of Falsehood*, *SBT*, Ser. 2, No. 16 (Allenson 1970).

5. C. Westermann, "The Way of Promise through the Old Testament," *The Old Testament and Christian Faith*, ed. B. Anderson (Herder and Herder 1969) 200–224.

6. H. W. Wolff, "The Understanding of History in the Old Testament Prophets," *Essays on Old Testament Hermeneutics*, ed. C. Westermann (John Knox Press 1963) 336–355.

7. C. Stuhlmueller, *Creative Redemption in Deuteronomy–Isaiah*, An Bib XLIII (1970).

4
The Way of Justice

A major feature in the contemporary scholarship on the prophets is the recognition of their earth boundedness. Although the prophets were different personalities and each one brought his or her own history and traditions, a common trait is their uncanny ability to look reality straight in the eye. There was the temptation, no doubt, to speak so as to please their hearers and, at times, it would have been easier just to get on the bandwagon and parrot the old cliches. Nevertheless, we find in the prophets a realism, a concern with the pots and pans of life, which leaves us dumbfounded and feeling awkward in our clinical, suburban and very controlled definition of religion as church-going.

Nowhere is the realism of the prophets more evident than in what we can term their social concern, which is a thread joining many themes together.

The Prophets Embrace God's Point of View

The social consciousness of the sixties brought about for us an immense appreciation of how the prophets involved themselves in interpreting the causes and underlying structures of the corrupt, socio-economic and political life of their day. They were not, however, social reformers *per se*. One would look in vain for the prototype of Saul Alinsky in their midst. The difference is one of origins. They came from the awesome experience of the judgment of God to view the phenomenon of people's lives together. We might say that they challenged the mythical basis of the economic life of the people. The ideology and evaluation which undergirded society's accepted structure into certain classes of people, the haves and the have nots, was critiqued over against the democracy and egalitarianism inherent in being God's chosen people. For example, in an extraordinary way the prophet entered into refashioning the ideology which undergirds Israel's kingship and its modifications to validate the respective thrones in the North and South. Already in the time of David, Nathan placed the understanding of kingship within the perspective of the Sinai covenant when he challenged David's unjust treatment of his subject. By way of another example, we can cite the fact that the separation of the North from the South in 921 B.C. was sanctioned by the prophet Ahijah of Shiloh as protest against Rehoboam's practices (I King 11–12) against the demands of social justice.

Forging Fundamental and Indivisible Options

The prophets were conscious, above all else, of the interconnectedness of Israel's sin, in the words of

Jeremiah, Israel's "rebellion." They backed Israel up against the wall, so to speak, and refused any superficial or piecemeal solution. In face of God's coming judgment, it was deemed an unwarranted luxury to try to "fix" Israel's problems, to bandaid Israel's wounds. The prophets would prepare Israel to meet God, preclude any space to execute an easy escape, and decry the people's willingness to engage in cheap grace, for instance, a ritualistic sort of playing games with lamentation and repentance. Either Israel would be met in all the spheres of life or face the fact of its total infidelity across the board, symptomized in any one of the social, economic, political or religious settings. In demanding of Israel such a total and indivisible response, the prophets embodied the jealousy of God who would tolerate no rival and whose claims were all or nothing. This ability of the prophets to relate sinfulness experienced in many spheres to the one core rebelliousness in the heart of Israel aided the prophets in convincing the community of its total inability to redress this situation out of its own resources, out of reliance on itself. This view of the interwoveness of the prophetic judgments can help us make sense of their utterances and especially in their present canonical shape. So often it might seem that the words of the prophets have been edited in a haphazard fashion. But once we have placed our finger on the links which result in the prophets' wholistic viewpoint, their overwhelming conviction is borne out that no human is righteous of him or herself before God.

Before proceeding to expose from the prophetic

texts the series of observations on which these preceding paragraphs are founded, two observations are in order. Firstly, it is good to note that we can detect in each prophet an expression characteristic of each one's assessment of this sinfulness, an interwovenness of the many attitudes and actions which miss the point of God's freely-offered, covenanted relationship. For example, Hosea speaks of the "spirit of harlotry which has led them (Israel) astray" (4:12); Isaiah sums up his indictment as a crisis of faith in the Holy One of Israel (cf. 7:9); Jeremiah, as noted earlier, detected rebelliousness. "Why do these people rebel with obstinate resistance?" (8:5); and Ezechiel, using language similar to that to be used by the priestly author in Genesis, speaks of "lawlessness. . . . in full bloom; flourishing insolence" (7:10).

Secondly, we need to note the conversion to which the people are called. The love which can sustain such an avalanche of sinfulness must be a great love indeed, and the conversion urged is a sincere turning back, not to one's own perceived rules of right conduct, but conversion to the person and will of the one who calls (compare a similar understanding of Paul in Romans 9:6–18). Such love is not beyond a certain repentance and self-searching itself, so intense is the pain and anguish of much betrayal. We can listen to the words of Micah (6:3–4).

> "O my people, what have I done to you,
> or how have I wearied you? Answer me!

> For I brought you up from the land of
>   Egypt,
> from the place of slavery I release you;
> And I sent before you Moses, Aaron and
>   Miriam."

We hear another outpouring (from Second Isaiah,
54:7–10) of this love and with it an assurance to undo
the chaos of sin and redo creation.

> "In an outburst of wrath, for a moment
> I hid my face from you;
> But with enduring love, I take pity on you,
> says the Lord, your Redeemer.

> "This is for me like the days of Noah when I
> swore that the waters of Noah should
> never again deluge the earth; so I have
> sworn not to be angry with you,
> or to rebuke you.

> "Though the mountains leave their place
> and the hills be shaken,
> My love shall never leave you or my
> covenant of peace be shaken,
> says the Lord who has mercy on you."

"Word Processing" Heightens Awareness of Sin

The "word processing" enterprise is one of our
fastest growing service industries today. The phrase

"word processing" is an evocative image to describe what went on in the prophetic ministry. Of course, it was less the *techniques* of word processing which engendered the message of the prophets than it was the *power impact* of their word which necessitated a more versatile structure of language, elicited a more articulate recall, and provoked a wider dissemination. If we extend the word processing image to include the use of television and movies, then we can compare yet another phenomenon of our times with an activity of the prophets. In recent years these media have placed before us in capsule form the atrocities of the 20th century, the unequalled inhumanity of human beings against each other within the lifetime of the majority of the world's population. When patterns of evil are so clearly delineated, attempts to water down individual acts of evil are seen as stalling tactics and evasive of reality. The phenomenon of prophecy had something of a similar revelatory force in Israel's self-perception.

It is our contention that the words of the prophets cumulatively taken cumulatively reveal emerging patterns in Israel's life with its covenanted Lord. No one prophet says it all, but the testimony of many prophets and the creative handing on of their words causes many pieces to fall together in assembling the details of Israel's non-response to God. We appreciate the ministry of the prophets on the pre-literary, oral level when we build in many elements of the situation and thus recapture the totality of their presentations. Although our reconstruction at times can be too fanciful, nevertheless, the effort is necessary because literature by itself cannot ever retrieve all the nuances which were shared by speakers and hearers. Oftentimes, such an effort leads to new discoveries, as, for instance, when we "contextualize" the vineyard song of Isaiah 5 or the put down of harvest celebrating in Hosea 9. This exercise of imaginatively overcoming the distance between the details of the original hearers and the quite differently situated modern reader is not always easy. For example, it becomes difficult when we try to make up our minds whether Jeremiah's confessions are wholly individual, reflect the language of the temple mourner, or, derived from the rite of being formally commissioned to be a prophet.[1] Words are incomparably alive in their own time and setting. But words are also social entities. When reinforced by facts of history, and reheard in the work of a prophet's disciples and especially when they are found to still "ring true," they take on "a life of their own." They become instruments of discernment in Israel's life; arising out of events in the past, these words disclose new dimensions to life in the present. Patterns of growth and ungrowth are set out in revelatory clarity when the prophets' words are repeated and really taken in and digested. We truly appreciate the ministry of the prophets on the canonical level when we are alive to the retention of individuals' names and dates and occasions of speaking God's Word and yet are attentive to the new position and perspectives gained as the text collaborates with and complements the surrounding material. The editor of these remembered words has been accountable to the history of the word's perceived importance without, however, limiting the editor's skill and creativity.[2] These theoretical observations will become alive and relevant if we now turn our attention to the woe oracles in the prophets, one of the major bearers of the social justice concerns of the prophets.

Woe-Oracles: Preliminary Remarks [3]

In staking out the original setting of these oracles, we run into some rough terrain. The prophets were so free in taking over language for their own purposes that the precise nuances which they would have us catch in how they use a particular form is not easy to discern. Scholars are undecided on the original situation in life which furnishes these forms. Are woe-oracles originally at home in the process of handing on of wisdom? Or are they originally at home in the rites of a funeral? Should we not, perhaps, distinguish between the origin and the use of a form? As an example from another branch of Old Testament research, we might point to the "Thou shalt not" form of the Ten Commandments. These are clear-cut, unconditional, policy-setting dictates said to be in *apodictic* as opposed to *casuistic* form. Their form may very well be found originally in the handing on of experience-based wise observations to a young person at the outset of new adventure and risk taking. If this suggestion should answer the question of the origin of the form, then a second question is the present use of this form in the Ten Commandments and what relationship exists between the origin and the use. Was there a cultic use in the Ten Commandments' employment of the form and would not Israel have found itself at crossroads with the moment of covenant renewal at hand?

The discussion of the woe-oracles might likewise be handled along the lines of origin and use. There is good reason to believe that these oracles owe their origin to the kind of fence which ancient wisdom built about certain actions because they were fraught with ominous outcomes. The forces of death invaded living space when the actions proscribed were not totally shunned. Such had happened before; why not again? A word to the wise is sufficient! When, therefore, the prophets use these woe-oracles, where are they standing? Are they threatening Israel with what might be, or are they attending the funeral rites of one already defunct: "She is fallen, to rise no more, the virgin Israel; she lies abandoned upon her land, with no one to raise her up" (Amos 5:2).

Are we to argue then to a creative use by the prophet of this form which had its origin in wisdom circles? We would understand, of course, that that origin is never totally eclipsed. We must go further because the real impact of these oracles as used by the prophets is contained now in their redactional whole. The pattern of death revealed to be at the core of Israel's life is devastatingly exposed in the redactor's lining up of the oracles as, for instance, in Isaiah 5:8–23. Within the framework of the series of woes, we can comprehend all the more the interconnectedness of Israel's sin on the social, economic, political and religious levels. We will look at some of these oracles now and perceive not only their unconditional forthrightness, but also their realism in confronting Israel with its wrong-doing and evil ways.

Woe-Oracles in Isaiah

The collection of woe-oracles which appears in Isaiah 5:8–23 is continued in 10:1–4. This part of the book of Isaiah, Chapters 1–12, admits of many conjectures as to how its redactional wholeness was achieved. The three-chapter break in the woe-oracles indicates that this series may have been a continuous unit previous to the insertion of the material of Chapter 6–9. The scope of our reflections prevents a further elucidation here, but the facts mentioned indicate enough to appreciate the interlocking of sections on weal and woe as the text assumes its final shape and content.

Isaiah 5:8–20
[8]Woe to those who join house to
house,
who add field to field,
until there is no more room,
and you are made to dwell alone
in the midst of the land.
[9]The LORD of hosts has sworn in my
hearing:
"Surely many houses shall be
desolate,

large and beautiful houses,
    without inhabitant.
[10]For ten acres of vineyard shall yield
    but one bath,
and a homer of seed shall yield
    but an ephah."

[11]Woe to those who rise early in the
    morning,
that they may run after strong
    drink,
who tarry late into the evening
    till wine inflames them!
[12]They have lyre and harp,
    timbrel and flute and wine at their
    feasts;
but they do not regard the deeds of
the LORD,
or see the work of his hands.

[13]Therefore my people go into exile
    for want of knowledge;
their honored men are dying of
    hunger,
and their multitutde is parched with
    thirst.
[14]Therefore Sheol has enlarged its
    appetite
and opened its mouth beyond
    measure,
and the nobility of Jerusalem and

her multitude go down,
her throng and he who exults in
her.
[15]Man is bowed down, and men are
brought low,
and the eyes of the haughty are
humbled.
[16]But the LORD of hosts is exalted in
justice.
and the Holy God shows
himself holy in righteousness.
[17]Then shall the lambs graze as in
their pasture,
fatlings and kids shall feed among
the ruins.

[18]Woe to those who draw iniquity
with cords of falsehood,
who draw sin as with cart ropes,
[19]who say: "Let him make haste,
let him speed his work
that we may see it;
let the purpose of the Holy One of
Israel draw near,
and let it come, that we may know
it!"

[20]Woe to those who call evil good
and good evil,
who put darkness for light
and light for darkness,

who put bitter for sweet
and sweet for bitter!

The series is led off with a rather lenghty oracle
in 5:8–10 which shares with judgment speeches the
twofold phenomenon of mentioning a crime and as-
signing a punishment. The crime is very obviously a
common occurrence. One can detect in the simple and
direct language the practice of building monopolies, or
translated into modern parlance, congolomerates at
the expense of the poor. Vs. 9 introduces God's reaction to the situation and the following verses indicate a
punishment without specifying a personal agent. Nature itself will react. Greed leads to its own infertility.
It is quite remarkable how often the prophets envision
the reaction, indeed, as it were, the recoiling of nature
in face of mankind's ungrateful misuse. This dimension will engage our attention at a later stage.

The next woe-oracle in 5:11–17 is an enlarged literary form with what seems like additions in verse 13
and verse 14, respectively, and a resumption in verse
15. Verse 16 sounds like a concluding refrain. The
woe-oracle itself addresses those who indulge in drinking "strong drink" and wine to excess precisely because they thus disregard what the Lord does. "The
work of His hands they see not." If we explore the
meaning of this word "work" as it is applied to God in
Isaiah, a very revealing meaning is obtained. What we
term history is known as God's "work" in Isaiah. This
oracle then concerns the blindness of the leaders,
brought about by excessive drinking which prevents

them from perceiving the options open to them in the
political arena of their day. The prophet himself offered an option which demanded deep faith in Yahweh
and an entrusting of Israel to the designs of the Lord
in how the nation would respond to the threat of the
combined strategy of the Northern Kingdom and of
Syria. We may not be much off the mark to suggest
that this oracle contains the prophet's doom against
the blindness which leads the leaders to reject the
prophet's faith interpretation of the threat experienced
in the political events of the years 735–733 B.C. It is
interesting to note how Chapter 28 offers a similar argument about excessive drinking an abuse which led
to deriding the prophet.

The meaning of the imagery in the opening verse
of the next woe-oracle (vv. 18–19) is not easily figured
out. Perhaps, the prophet is thinking of the energy
with which the so-called wise men of Jerusalen, those
on the King's advisory board, seek out and hold on te-
naciously to their sinfulness. One is reminded of the
very bold imagery of Jeremiah where he discusses Israel's fascination with the irresistible attractiveness of
sin. He considers Israel's activity as that of a "frenzied
she-camel, coursing near and far, breaking away to-
ward the desert, snuffing the wind in her ardor—who
can restrain her lust?" (2:23–24). The Good News Bible translates the opening line of the oracle in Isaiah,
5:18 as follows:

"You are doomed! You are unable to break free
from your sins." Of whom has such a heavy description been used? As if not to add or subtract from the

perversity of their sin, the prophet cites these persons'
own words:

> "Let him make haste and speed his work
> that we might see it. On with the plan of the
> Holy One of Israel, let it come to pass, that
> we may know it!"

What incredible arrogance! Would not these words
have been addressed to the prophet himself since he
presented himself as spokesman for God's plan within
Israel's historical horizon? But their quoted words
make great irony. In tempting the Lord to demonstrate his plan before they will consent to believe, they
show their self-designated wisdom to be no other than
the stupidity of a tethered beast of burden for which
no options exist. This woe runs to the heart of Isaiah's
message. He constantly confronted the councillors of
the King with their lack of enlightenment. These persons have ignored the reality that God, too, is wise
(see 30:1–5, 31:1–3) and the perversity of their guilt is
found in their refusal to entertain other points of view.
Another woe-oracle of Isaiah comes to mind (29:15)
where again these truly foolish ones are indicted in
their own words:

> "Woe to those who would hide their plans
> too deep for the Lord! Who work in the
> dark, saying, 'who sees us, or who knows
> us?' "

The last woe-oracle which we will consider here, Isaiah 5:20, regards the condition in which those persons condemned in the previous oracles, find themselves. Those who would test God by demanding demonstrations of his effectiveness now move into total moral utilitarianism. They turn things upside down as the antithetical word pairs, good/evil, darkness/light, bitter/sweet demonstrate so well. A moral bankruptcy has incapacitated the leaders. They have rendered themselves unavailable to the word of the prophet. One scholar has suggested that this oracle echoes the sin of the first parents. They want to determine what is good and what is evil. The root of both the sins of the wise men of Jerusalem and of the first parents, is the same: the perverse questioning of the wisdom of God in creation and in history. Two woe-oracles in Second Isaiah very bluntly state the unnaturalness of this perversity (45:9–10):

"Woe to him who contends with his Maker;
a potsherd among potsherds of the earth!
Does the clay say to its modeler, 'What are you doing?' or, 'What you are making has no hands?'

Woe to him who asks a father, 'What are you begetting?' or a woman, 'What are you giving birth to?' "

As we study these woe-oracles, we can note a shift in their content, while their basic form remains the same. It would seem that their content is concerned, at first, with economic social matters, then expands to include Israel's opaqueness in face of God's plans in history and finally questions the adequacy of Israel's self-definition as even a religious people. When the prophets upbraid Israel's sinfulness, they are not picayune over minor transgressions, but indicating the indivisibility of the total waywardness into which Israel has willingly and woefully strayed.

The Unnaturalness of Israel's Sins

If the study of the woe-oracles opens vistas on the interconnectedness of sin in Israel's life, it points also to sin's unnaturalness as a primary concern of the prophets. We have indicated the influence of wisdom and now we need to explore for a while the broadening of wisdom concerns into concerns of theodicy, or rather, into those concerns which we would classify under the category of theodicy. This direction in our study discloses new insights into the conceptual framework of the prophets and at times the logic of their argumentation. We might begin our reflection on the appeal to wisdom as akin to our appeal in argumentation to common sense. Thus Isaiah's words:

> "An ox knows its owner,
> and an ass its master's manger;

but Israel does not know,
my people has not understood." (1:3)

On a deeper level the prophets, in using wisdom motifs, touch the people's faith in God as creator. If only the people would learn from nature, they would know the patterns of God's activity. It is the one God who speaks in history and acts in creation. Should not the wise men of Jerusalem learn the ways of God in history just as the farmer learns the ways of God in creation and thus knows when to sow, plough and reap? The argument is cogently presented in Isaiah 28:23–29 and the final verse reads:

"This too comes from the Lord of hosts;
wonderful is his counsel and great his wisdom."

Within the description of what the farmer does, one verse (26) intervenes between the questions and the answers. The New American Bible translation reads thus:

"He has learned this rule
instructed by his God."

The word "rule" translates the Hebrew word *mishpat*. This is one of the most powerful words in the Hebrew scriptures and admits of many shades of meaning.[4] It is often translated "justice" and is often in the same context with *sedeqah* which can be rendered "righteousness." Thus, for example, in discussing what genuine cult is all about, Amos has Yahweh say:

> "Away with your noisy songs!
> I will not listen to the melodies of your
>   harps.
> But if you would offer me holocausts,
> then let justice (*mishpat*) surge like water,
> and goodness (*sedeqah*) like an unfailing
>   stream." (5:23–24)

This justice is something which touches the life of a man in relationships with his neighbors—the alien, the orphan, the widow—but it also touches the rule of cosmic harmony which God as Creator has placed in creation. In an argument resembling that of Isaiah considered above, Jeremiah states:

> "Even the stork in the air
> knows its seasons;
> Turtledove, swallow and thrush
> observe their time of return,
> but my people do not know
> the *mishpat* (ordinance) of the Lord." (8:7)

If God is presented as coming in judgment against the people, it is to redress the injustice, the abuse of the interrelationship of all things in creation which makes the universe an enduring and fuctioning entity. The art of creation is a tedious task, and God's justice is part of that arduous withholding of the waters of chaos. What is so terrible and horrifying about sin upon sin in people's lives is that that delicate balance is ever being upset and the presence of the Creator is defied.

The Role of the Servant in the Pursuit of Justice

We have traced a number of different threads so far and it might be well if we recapture the development. The argument is that the Old Testament prophets were inaugurating God's judgment against the people. When pressed to explain the factors in God's declared war against Israel, the prophets peered more deeply at the state of their nation's affairs. Social injustice appeared as a grave sin in Israel, but on closer inspection it was not just a case of isolated acts, but a whole disregard for the kind of God whom they had experienced Yahweh to be. The prophets' reflection moved beyond this contagion in sin to realize that disrespect for and violation of the social justice due one's neighbor was disrespect for and violation of the harmony which God had placed in the order of creation.

Here the prophets face the implications of Israel's covenant relationship with Yahweh. The questions which confronted the ancients and in response to which they produced creation myths were the questions, "who created us?" and the more important question "who will continue to give us fruitfulness and life?"[5] A vibrant and living faith in the God of the Exodus ultimately provided points of view that would help Israel give satisfactory answers to these existential questions. Thus, if the laws of the covenant (e.g. Ex. 20–23) touched significantly those same spheres of life, those existential questions of life and survival normally covered by the creation mythologies of other peoples, then pursuit of justice seen as the purpose of these laws lead into the whole area of creation theology. The laws not only developed a relationship to the national deity as rescuer out of Egypt, but also opened the people's lives to faith in this Yahweh as creator of all things. One will perhaps see something of this merger of understandings already in the ancient hymn in Exodus 15 extolling Yahweh for the victory over Pharoah. But the ministry of the prophets heightened the question as we have seen, because they pursued questions to their roots.

What the faith of Israel then had to offer was not only a salvation history, but faith in a creator God. This kind of synthesis is had in many texts in the Hebrew scriptures, not least in the juxtaposition of Genesis 1-11 and the remainder of the Pentateuch. In a very special way, however, the time of the Exile called forth the best in Israel's theology. If there could be a new beginning after the total destruction of the Exile that would have to be an initiative of love on the part of the creator-saviour God! It is no surprise to find that the new Exodus is depicted in Second Isaiah in new creation language. It would be wholly inadequate to see this "creative redemption" as just a poetic way of describing the new reality. In fact, what is ushered in and given considerable depth is a whole new way of celebrating faith in the Creator God of Love. It would take us too far afield to explore this development in its relationship to the polemic against the other gods, a theme vigorously delineated in Second Isaiah but certainly not for the first time in the prophets.

What we have then is really a new way of defining faith in God as Creator. The inner meaning of created reality is disclosed within the ambit of faith in God as savior, and thus God's saving activity is capable of being seen as part of God's creative activity. After the prophet's introduction and call in Second Isaiah, the next verses pose profound questions:

> "Who has cupped in his hands the waters of
>   the sea,
> and marked off the heavens with a span?
> Who has held in a measure the dust of the
>   earth,
> weighed the mountains in scales
> and the hills in a balance?
> Who has directed the spirit of the Lord,
> or has instructed him as his counsellor?
> Whom did he consult to gain knowledge?
> Who taught him the path of *mishpat*,
> or showed him the way of understanding?"
>   (40:12–14)

The focal point where both these expressions of faith, namely, that of God as Creator and that of God as Savior, come together is justice. Earlier, we established the meaning of the Suffering Servant as Israel, the prophetically depicted embodiment of Yahweh's plan arising out of long reflection on the prophet as one who bears the lot of the Word of God. Now, it will come as no surprise that the task of the Servant is to pursue justice. This is apparent many times in the reading of Isaiah 42:1–9. What needs to be stressed is that it is God's justice which is pursued and the servant is immensely privileged to be so drawn into the creative task of God's love. One is reminded here of a typically Proto-Isaian verse with which we will conclude this section:

> "But the Lord of Hosts shall be exalted by
>   his judgment,
> and God the Holy shall be shown holy by his
>   justice." (5:16)

Monotheistic Faith

The prophets revealed God to Israel. It was common to say in earlier scholarship that the prophets led Israel to a speculative monotheism, the well argued out position that there is only one God. This was spoken of in distinction from practical monotheism which purportly stated that "while there may be other gods, only one God has worked for us." Many times the speculative monotheism was tied in with the work of Second Isaiah, which, judging from the number of times we have gone there in these pages, was a climatic point in the development of the Old Testament religion in our view. We ought to be careful, however, because the distinction of practical and speculative monotheism is a very modern safety valve. It may be too simple a description of the past. It is true that the prophets moved Israel to a much clearer and more demanding appropriation of Yahweh's oneness. This unity of God was never worked out systematically. However, when a student of the prophetic literature keeps within the conceptual frameworks of the materials and does not impose outside categories and expectations, then the development of their thinking is very evident. That Yahweh is zealous and one and that the divine love is undivided was a conviction underlying all the prophets. As we thread our way on any given theme in the prophetic canon, we find ourselves confronted again and again as they were themselves with the reality of God's oneness. There is nothing wishy-washy about Yahweh and any polytheism or dualism is an unrealistic option. The prophets were Israel's reality therapists and their approach called for the deepest integration. The approach can be called justice and bespoke the living out in covenanted response the kind of love with which Yahweh redemptively and creatively loves Israel.

NOTES

1. John Bright, "Jeremiah's Complaints: Liturgy or Expressions of Personal Distress?" *Proclamation and Presence*, eds. J. I. Durham and J. R. Porter (SCM 1970) 189–214.

2. For a helpful understanding of the transition from word as spoken to Word of God as written see R. E. Mur-

phy, "The Old Testament as Word of God," *A Light unto my Path*, pp. 363–374.

3. J. W. Whedbee, *Isaiah and Wisdom* (Abingdon 1971).

4. Eliezer Berkovits, "The Biblical Meaning of Justice," *Judaism*, 18:188–207 (1969).

5. L. Fisher, "Creation at Ugarit and in the Old Testament," *VT* 15:313–324 (1965).

6. Recent discussion of the Pauline notion of God's righteousness as embrasive also of creation motifs beyond salvation motifs does very well to draw from Second Isaiah at this point. For an overview of the current discussion see M. T. Brauch's appendix in E. P. Sanders, *Paul and Palestinian Judaism. A Comparison of Patterns of Religion* (Fortress 1977).

5
A Prophet in Their Midst

In what sense is Israelite prophecy unique? As long as we are willing to study the identity of the prophets "from below" we cannot claim a total uniqueness for them. The phenomenon of prophecy in Israel must be assessed over against the evidence for prophecy elsewhere but especially in the ancient Near East. Nowhere else outside Israel, however, do we find the same quantity or quality of material on either individual prophets or the phenomenon of prophecy as such. In fact, it is somewhat unscientific to predicate the word prophecy of similar phenomena in whole or in part from other lands and cultures because our expectations of finding similarities are conditioned by the immense impression of the Israelite data. The many centuries of both the early and later prophets, however, were not times of a consistent phenomenon holding up under all sorts of ups and downs. In fact, the Scriptures do little to hide evidence of the diverse origins of prophecy. Even a preliminary reading of the prophetic corpus convinces the reader that this access to the knowledge of a deity was not a uniform religious undertaking. There was growth and development, weakening and ultimately a demise. It is possible, however, to relate many individual aspects of prophecy in Israel with evidence of similar aspects elsewhere, whether in Canaan, Phoenicia, Egypt or Mari.[1]

The closest example of many elements in common with Israel's prophetic heritage is that of Mari, in ancient Mesopotamia, today an archaeological site in modern Syria. The ancient royal archives dating back to 1800–1760 B.C.E. yielded many cuneiform tablets which were composed in Akkadian. Indications are that the ruling class was of West Semitic origin. Huffmon in his IDBS article notes that the mixed cultural milieu of the texts has many ties with the Hebrew patriarchs and with early Israel. He proceeds to discuss the data on prophecy from Mari under many headings, for instance, speakers with and without titles, the setting of the oracles, the presence or absence of cultic overtones, the place of the king as recipient of prophetic messages, etc. The Mari prophets have been noted by other scholars to resemble royal messengers or ambassadors of the gods to the local rulers.[2] Wifall notes that their messages were couched in formulas similar to the divine speeches to Israel in the Hebrew Scriptures. The conclusion, however, of a dissertation recently published is that although parallels are to be conceded, there was no unified phenomenon of prophecy at Mari which can be brought to bear on that of Israel as illustrative of the latter's pre-history.[3] It should also be remembered that we do not have in any fashion sufficient material from Mari over a length of time to plot a trajectory of the origin and development of prophecy there. This we certainly have from Israel. It is the juxtaposition of so many elements in Israel which is truly unique and the impression that this results from the uniqueness of the God of Israel ingratiates itself more and more on the researcher's mind. There is mention of one phenomenon in Mari which may be very indicative of the social reality of prophecy there which again differentiates it from the claim to authority which the social reality of prophecy had in the society of Israel. Often a lock of hair or a snip of the hem of the speaker's garment was requested to accompany the prophet's report, presumably, writes Huffmon, to function as some kind of technical divination. No such go-between was allowed in Israel where, on the contrary, the prophets were increasingly seen as personally responsible for their own words.

Can We Find a Model for the Prophets?

In discussing the shift from pre-classical prophets to classical prophets in the Introduction, we indicated the impact of social and historical realities on the perception of the prophet. The prophet became more clearly a public person if not also, in fact, an international personage. Our knowledge of that shift was based on our study of the text especially in its canonical form. Scholarship must trace the shifts in the models used to describe the prophets only on the basis of the textual data before us, or at least begin the discus-

sion of the various models from the text and only sub-
sequently employ data from history or sociology.
Previously we set aside, therefore, the question of the
prophet as creator of Israel's ethical monotheism because it began in modern polemics and searched for
subsequent verification in the text. It would seem also
that shifts in the consciousness of Israel as to who are
its prophets should be related to historical change and
be themselves interrelated. No one model is adequate
to explain who is the prophet vis-à-vis Yahweh and
vis-à-vis Israel throughout the entire period. Neither,
of course, was there but one image of who Yahweh is
to the people of Israel. The language about Yahweh
had to shift often in order to accommodate continuity of
faith in a God who remained faithful. We can speak of
Yahweh as kinsman, overlord, spouse, king, warrior,
international ruler, farmer, father and mother.

There are some images which bear up through
many changes. One might point to Yahweh as warrior. This is not a very popular image for God among
modern people, but in the eyes of the ancient Israelites
much of their hope for the future was grounded in
their experience of God as Warrior, who continues to
lead the battle against the forces of uncreation, chaos
and injustice.[4] In the context of Yahweh as warrior,
scholarship has attempted to trace the history of the
war oracle in the prophets. Being a God who fights for
his people against others, Yahweh at times declares
war on Israel who has spurned the covenant obliga-
tions. But God will also lead Israel into the battle of
the eschatological times. The war oracle of the pre-

classical period gives way to the judgment speech of the classical period and evolves eventually into the language of early apocalyptic. A trajectory within the evolution of the language can be intuited perhaps more often than rigorously demonstrated. It may be noted in passing that, while the general thrust of such research cannot be gainsaid, the actual case of such evolution demands rigorous scientific controls.[5]

A not unrelated image of the prophet is that of prosecutor, the one who takes Israel to court on charges of covenant infidelity. One scholar has attempted to link this role of the prophet with the function of messenger and speaks of the angel prophet and satan prophet, the messenger and prosecutor.[6] Just how extensive this image of lawyer is in the language of the prophets is debatable. On the one hand, there is a development within the judgment speeches, an expansion to include more people, describe the punishments more articulately, and involve wider charges, not merely of disobedience, but of total abandonment of the covenant. Compare, for instance, judgment speeches in the former prophets in Amos and in the opening chapters of Jeremiah.[7] On the other hand, the specifically forensic language of what is known as the Rib pattern (Is 1:2–3; 3:13–15; Hosea 4:1–3 and others) becomes a very special commodity in the hands of the prophets. This development of language is clearly evident when Second Isaiah can use this pattern, not to prosecute Israel for breach of covenant, but to argue that Yahweh is Lord of history.

Now the Lord calls the nations and their divine

leaders to explain the outcome of history. This use of forensic language should not be construed to claim that Israel's religion was legalistic, but rather to express Israel's conviction that Yahweh was not capricious. The Semitic mind set finds in this language a way to express the firmly held belief, in no way cheaply arrived at, that Yahweh was a God of order and plan and could be counted on for fidelity in matters of supreme importance and of universal scope. In making these remarks one cannot but be reminded of the Rib pattern which precipitates the major showdown in the book of Job, and which indeed leads to Job's tranformation into the plan and wisdom of God. This mention of Job may be enough to indicate that one must cautiously seek the original situation in life of the prophets' use of legal language. Was the language "at home" in the justice practiced at the city gate, or in the cultic celebration of the covenant or in the practice of international law? Or should we find adequate explanation of the prophets' appropriation of this legal language in the law-oriented mind set of the Semites?

These questions lead us to consider yet another image of God and the corresponding prophetic model, that of Yahweh as covenant overlord and the prophet as covenant mediator. The scholarship of the recent past has brought a lot of light to bear on these questions. The matter had been obscured by arguments and counter-arguments arising from the Wellhausen approach being opposed by the American archaeological approach. If Wellhausen, using Hegelian philosophy, tended to view early Israel as having had a primitive expression of religion which was antithesized in the ethical monotheism of the prophets, the American approach was to find perhaps too much of the later prophetic religion in the very beginnings of Mosaic Religion. A heightened covenant theology articulated in terms of international treaties—depicting Yahweh as overlord and Israel as vassal—is perhaps not evidenced till the early phases of the so-called Deuteronomic movement.[8] To claim that the prophets were mediators of this Yahweh-Israel relationship is not incorrect, but to derive it from the language of international treaty making in Mosaic times is far less secure. That there was a covenant understanding of the Sinaitic experience is clear, but that this relationship was conceptualized according to the treaty formulary used between nations in the 2nd millennium has been disproved.

The language of Israel's relationship with God admitted of great diversity from the very beginning. Much of the religious, political and sociological underpinnings of this diversity would be lost to our view were we to impose on this language just one rigid model of covenant. In fact, the eventual employment of treaty formularies may well presuppose the presence of monarchy in Israel over a long period of time. This observation then heightens the tension with which Israel absorbed the language of kingship to articulate faith in Yahweh. This sets in much richer perspective the question of the origin of kingship in Israel and the prophetic struggle with the introduction of so alien a political system. The arguments against king-

ship may not be a reading into earlier times of understandings only gained post factum (see I Samuel 8) but
could well represent prophetic apprehension that the
trappings of kingship and *ab initio* violate something
of the very "democratic" or egalitarian character of Israel's early social understanding.

A new element in evaluation of the position of the
prophet vis-à-vis the king is the Egyptian connection.
Scholars assess differently the impact of Egypt on the
social, political and religious thinking of Israel.
George Mendenhall, for instance, has depicted the
conquest of Palestine as the work of internal revolu-
tion against Egyptian overlords triggered and enlight-
ened by the social ramifications of the newly found
faith in Yahweh, the God of the Hebrews.[9] Nevertheless, other scholars see the best model for the prophets
in the Egyptian Pharaoh's messengers not only to for-
eign courts, but also to his own vassals. If Israel must
have a king, then an older understanding of Yahweh
as king was taken up and finessed along Egyptian lines
in such a way that David was the prince and anointed
to office by the King's messenger, the prophet. Another opinion would see the prophet as absorbing the
role of Egyptian vizier, the supreme householder. In
whatever way all these ideas are worked out from the
available data, an important conviction emerges. Later
Israel would not only absorb kingship, but would articulate the relationship it enjoyed with God in the ex-
tended language of international kingships and treaties
and here we see the real force of the prophets as covenant mediators and the groundwork for yet another

model. Given the radical historical character of Israel's revealed religion, the prophets many times gave Israel the reflection and space to be syncretistic precisely by objecting to it. In being antisyncretistic the prophets faciliated the process of syncretism which must be so much a part of a religion borne through historical shifts. The *raison d'etre* of Israel was the covenanted relationship with God and the prophets facilitated this relationship as the generations passed through many epochs. The way this understanding might be expressed is to say that the prophets were the interior facilitators of the emerging self-consciousness of Israel as the people of God. People hunger for the effective language with which to interpret their human experience religiously. The prophets were ministers of the word because they provided Israel with that bold and effective language. It was a costly affair because they claimed for their interpretation the authority of the Word of God.

The Purpose of the Prophets

We live in the age of McDonald's and Burger King and in a world of a thousand other instant service industries. We live in a world of instant satisfaction. We have become suspicious of projects which take a very long time to achieve. In computerese we speak of "real" time. Never before has the world of the prophets seemed so far away; in our world of computerized experience, the generation gap exceeds by far the actual 2½ millennia differential. We are ourselves in the midst of very profound change in understanding our human condition and ambiguities galore abound. On the one hand, attention to historical record has intensified since the beginning of the modern period, and public figures often betray a paralyzing over-occupation with their place in history. On the other hand, the ignorance of history among the young is lamented by many educators. Nevertheless, a new search for one's roots has captured the present generation. How does one interpret the fact that thousands and thousands have crowded museums to see the Tutankhamen display? So there is a fascination with the past, an impetuosity with the present, a gradually deepening pessimism about the quality of the future. The pain of the future lies heavily upon us. It does not exist apart from our choosing it. The very technology which collapses past and future into the over-stimulation of the now, the "real" time, also informs us that the nuclear waste we are now burying will take one half million years to deactivate. We are confused and contradict ourselves. We live only for the now and we mess up the world and the opportunity of a future now for an estimated 500 millennia!

What can the prophets tell us about time and history and future? It is ridiculous to try capturing in one line what the prophets might have hoped would be their lasting impact. However, the following is an attempt: *time is on the side of those who love*. The explanation would run something like this. Only those who love can touch the meaning of time which in its profoundest significance is always time of meeting, of encounter and being with another, of shared and received presence. Those who love are alone those whose lives—in their coming and going, the beginning and the end, in sexuality and death—are received as gift. They are those who know they are loved, touched ultimately by divine passion, overwhelmed in the presence of the Holy One. The prophets thus intuited the dictum of the Psalmist that one day in the Lord's presence is worth a thousand elsewhere. For the prophets that one day of our human existence must be spent wholly on the side of the all holy God.[10] That day is spent in the striving midst of the human task but not ultimately in the defense of any one people or nation or land.

Israel from the beginning was very conscious of its own identity over against other peoples and other lands. The prophets used the language of judgment against the nations to bolster Israel's self-confidence. But as we move through the prophets, we discover a heightening awareness that these others also belong to Yahweh. The future will not be the accomplishment of any one nation but of all the peoples of the world engaged in the purposes of God. Is not this pattern in the prophets the paradigm of growth to integration and wholeness in the task and joy of being human? To move through all experiences and discover true identity is in belonging wholly to the purposes of God! The future is going out to meet the God who actively and effectively calls. That future is present time on the side of those who love. To live the present out of the grasp of this future—that is conversion! Conversion to God's willfulness, to God's "work" is how Isaiah would have phrased it. The prophet calls us to this conversion because the prophet is already caught up into God's timing; no prophet is self-called nor was the position hereditary. All are called and each one must leap. Jeremiah would say simply: one must have stood in the council of God—what a wonderful interpretation of our being made in the image and likeness of God! What is unique about the prophets is the uniqueness of the otherness who has drawn close and touched their lives. If this only happened to any one prophet, we could scoff and ask is not so and so also among the dreamers? But when there is a solid tradition, it is another story. And if these individuals support and strengthen each other, it is to introduce the moment, the timing of God in which they stand, to allow that timing to take hold and begin slowly to get us to perceive life from a faith point of view. Prophets are born to be losers—it is only after they are gone that we recall their words and see the pattern of their timing—their solos and harmonies—and are convinced that a prophet has been in our midst.

A final reflection on the Christian Community as prophetic presence to the world! Of course, this community finds its rootage in Jesus, the prophet of God who ushered in God's timing and who is wholly on the side of God. The one and the many—Jesus and the Christ, Jesus the prophet and the Christian Community—all of these vistas invite us to forego the limelight of being individually called prophet. Rather, we embody in the language event of our human existence the prophetic dimension of the Christian Gospel. To be in Christ is to belong to the prophet Jesus, who not only points to and articulates anew the plan of God, but is the very plan, the very mystery, the unfolding of God's design of love and compassion, the future.

NOTES

1. H. B. Huffmon, *IDBS*, 697–701; "The Origins of Prophecy," *Magnalia Dei: The Mighty Acts of God*, Frank M. Cross, et al, eds. (Garden City, N.J., Doubleday 1976); F. Moriarty, "Antecedents of Israelite Prophecy in the ANE," *Studia Missionalia* 22 (1973) 255–277.

2. W. Wifall, "A New Model for Prophecy," *The Bible Today*, 81:586–593 (December 1975); also see by the same author, *Israel's Prophets: Envoys of the King* (Herald Biblical Booklets: Franciscan Herald Press 1974).

3. E. Noort, *Untersuchungen zum Gottesbeschied in Mari: Die "Mariprophetie" in der Altestamentlichen Forschung*, (Neukirchener Verlag 1977): see *OTA*, 1:201–202 (1978).

4. G. E. Wright, *The Old Testament and Theology* (Harper and Row 1969).

5. Duane L. Christensen, *Transformation of the War Oracle in Old Testament Prophecy*, HTRHDR #3; Missoula, Mt: Scholars Press, 1978 (1975) reviewed by D. R. Hillers, *CBQ*, 40:89–91 (1978).

6. R. North, "Angel Prophet or Satan Prophet?" *ZAW*, 82:31–67 (1970).

7. C. Westermann, *Basic Forms of Prophetic Speech* (Westminster 1967); see also W. E. March, "Prophecy," *Old Testament Form Criticism*, ed. John Hayes (Trinity University Press 1974) pp. 141–177.

8. For a discussion of the state of the question see Dennis J. McCarthy, *Treaty and Covenant: A Study in Form*

in the Ancient Oriental Documents and in the Old Testament (An Bib 21A: Rome 1978). See also G. Mendenhall, "Samuel's Broken Rib," *No Famine in the Land*, Studies in honor of J. L. McKenzie eds. J. Flanagan and A. W. Robinson (Scholars Press 1975) pp. 63–74.

9. G. Mendenhall, *The Tenth Generation, The Origins of the Biblical Tradition* (Johns Hopkins 1973).

10. For complementary ideas consult P. M. George and Joseph D. Driskill, "Ancient Hebrew Religious Beliefs and the Evolution of Prophets," *Biblical Theology Bulletin*, 9:66–77 (1979).

Further Reading

Some introductory reading has been cited in the footnotes. The following list, however, is offered to assist the non-specialist in further reading. The listing is simply alphabetical in form with no attempt to prioritize. However, a short note is attached to each item which will hopefully help in making choices of works with which to begin one's own study.

Anderson, B. W., *The Eighth Century Prophets*, Amos, Hosea, Isaiah, Micah (Fortress 1978).
> This listing is offered as an example of Proclamation Commentaries—a series designed to assist the homilist which contains very worthwhile resumés of the findings of modern scholarship.

Beaucamp, Evode, O.F.M., *Prophetic Intervention in the History of Man* (Alba 1970).
> The title of the original French includes the word "election" and this is the perspective from which the universalism in the prophets is etched. A clearly written treatment of many individual prophets out of a holistic orientation.

Blenkinsopp, J., *Prophecy and Canon* (University of Notre Dame Press 1977).
> A study in canon criticism; its advantages over the criticisms to date and the major role played by the creative

tension between prophecy and tradition in the process of the Hebrew Scripture canon.

Bright, John, *Covenant and Promise* (Westminster 1976).
The subtitle is an instant clue: "The prophetic understanding of the future in pre-exilic Israel." Simply written, the work exhibits a very good handling of varying traditions in Israel's selfconsciousness.

Bruggemann, W., *Tradition for Crisis* (John Knox 1968).
A very worthwhile discussion of the theme of covenant in the theology of Hosea with special emphasis on the meaning of tradition. The detailed handling of many texts never leaves the non-specialist out of easy access to the text.

Bruggemann, W., *The Prophetic Imagination* (Fortress 1978).
The author discusses the great issue of ministry in our time out of the need to proceed with imagination—prophetic imagination. "The task of prophetic ministry is to nurture, nourish and evoke a consciousness and perception alternative to the consciousness and perception of the dominant culture about us."

Clements, R. E., *One Hundred Years of Old Testament Interpretation* (Westminster 1976).
This work provides background reading in the history of Old Testament interpretation which will help the reader of these pages to understand references to Wellhausen and other pivotal figures in the scholarship.

Clements, R. E., *Prophecy and Tradition* (John Knox 1975).
This volume appears in a series called, "Growing Points in Theology." The question of tradition is surely such a growing point. Out of a holistic appreciation, Clements' work is written to present new insights and connect exaggerations in earlier scholarship.

Corbett, J. Elliott, *The Prophets on Main Street* (John Knox 1978).

A provocative attempt to relate the message of the prophets to the issues of modern-day society. The work is worthwhile in its attempt to relate the totality of the age out of which the prophets emerged with the totality of the age in which they are heard anew. An exercise in the methodology of relativizing the message of the prophets!

Gottwald, N. K., *All the Kingdoms of the Earth*, Israelite Prophecy and International Relations in the Ancient Near East (Harper & Row 1964).

A classical study of the prophets as interpreters of the international situation in which they found themselves.

Hanson, P., *The Dawn of Apocalyptic* (Fortress 1975).

Hanson has written many articles on apocalyptic and especially in explanation of his own newer approach. This work assembles many of his studies; some are technical, others are quite comprehensible to the nonspecialist.

Heaton, E. W., *The Old Testament Prophets* (John Knox 1977).

A new edition which is virtually a new book! A very fine treatment of general topics and then prophets grouped in themes. The work is very informed on newer insights and approaches.

Heschel, A., *The Prophets* (Harper and Row Paperback, 1962 and 1971).

A classic! Together with the technical expert, we need also the poet in order to feel the pathos of God in the prophets. Truly a *vade mecum* from a modern Jewish scholar.

Holladay, W. L., *Isaiah: Scroll of a Prophetic Heritage* (Eerdmans 1978).

Presented in this listing here as an example of a popular commentary written out of deep sensitivity to the place of tradition and the community. This, of course, is to be eminently appreciated in Isaiah. See the same author's work on Jeremiah where the continuity is sustained in terms of person. Both works exhibit great attention to literary technique in the editorial work of the prophetic books. See then W. L. Holladay, *Jeremiah: Spokesman Out of Time* (United Church Press 1974).

Lindblom, J., *Prophecy in Ancient Israel* (Fortress 1962).

A very comprehensive work, considered a classic and reference point on many issues dealing with the phenomenon of prophecy. Also each prophet is considered under many headings.

von Rad, G., *Message of the Prophets* (Harper & Row 1967).

A breakthrough! von Rad's work—a distillation of the second volume of his famous Old Testament Theology—introduced the discussion of the prophet as the tradition person in ancient Israel. A point of departure on all modern discussions. Very accessible to the nonspecialist.

Scott, R. B. Y., *The Relevance of the Prophets* (MacMillian 1968).

A revised edition of a 1944 work! The work treats in ten chapters questions of prophecy in general—the phenomenon, antecedents, succession, word, etc. A classic exposition which has merited a new edition because of its width of discussion and immense clarity of expression.

Seilhamer, F., *Prophets and Prophecy* (Fortress 1977).

A series of short essays—devoted to seven key messengers—crisply written and very well informed on modern scholarship, addressed to a general audience.

Westermann, C., *Basic Forms of Prophetic Speech* (Westminster 1967).

Considered a classic! Westermann's famous exposition of the judgment speeches of the prophets. The first part is a technical discussion of the history of form critical research.

Winward, S. F., *A Guide to the Prophets* (paperback John Knox 1976).

A very reliable compact treatment of each prophet in the Hebrew Canon. The work includes a long discussion of introductory questions.

Other Books in This Series

From your bookstore or from
Paulist Press
545 Island Road
Ramsey, N.J. 07446